MW01245028

The Gyp Lease Tales
and Other Lies

The Gyp Lease Tales and Other Lies

WALT DAVIS

© 2017 Walt Davis
All rights reserved.

ISBN: 1979619107
ISBN 13: 9781979619103

The Gyp Lease

THE GYP LEASE was a seven-section – that's 4480 acres for those of you from east Texas – pasture located a little ways from Palava in Fisher County, Texas. The United States Gypsum Company bought this land years ago because it had a few feet of soil sitting on top of gypsum deposits a couple of hundred feet thick. To bring in a return on their investment until mining started, the company leased the land to area ranchers. With the lease being up for bids every few years, whoever held the lease tended to use all of the grass available and over the years, the grass declined and the mesquite brush increased. This was the situation until USG sold the land – someone in the company inventoried their deposits and realized that at their present rate of consumption they wouldn't run out of gypsum where they were currently mining for something like a thousand years. The one thing that is not in short supply in west Texas is gyp; it's in the water, in the soil and, during dust storms, in the air. The gyp lease was sold and the new owners started an improvement program sometime in the 1960's but at the time that I knew it, the gyp lease was seven square miles of solid mesquite brush with enough grass underneath to support a cow to about every twenty acres. The land was flat and cut with steep sided winding dry washes, no cross fences and no landmarks except a windmill in the southwest corner. The gypsum deposits were honey combed with sinkholes and underground caverns that were home to a very healthy population of rattlesnakes. There is a story in how and why the land called the gyp lease deteriorated so quickly – going from productive prairie grassland to brush thicket in one generation – but that will have to wait; this is a story not so much about the land but about the people and the times.

The Way Things Were

IN THE EARLY 1940's my Dad – Willis Davis – and Walter Boothe were partners on the gyp lease and had it stocked with 200 Hereford cows. Those seven sections were as the saying goes "a dammed good place to lose a cow"; the brush was 10-12 feet tall and so thick that anywhere you could see 100 feet was considered a clearing. It didn't take long for those Hereford cows to realize that they could get through the brush a lot faster than a man could horse back and that if they didn't want to go, he couldn't make them. Screwworms were still bad at this time and stock infected with this pest had to be treated or they would die. The constant chousing caused by the need to rope and doctor "wormies" didn't help make gentle cattle. One or two men could doctor wormies with enough riding, mainly because the horses could smell the worms and would go to an infected animal like a bird dog goes to quail, but it took a lot of help to pen the cattle.

The world was at war and many of the countries' young men were in uniform. The draft board issued exemptions for men deemed essential to food production but even without this exemption cowboys would still have been in fair supply. There were lots of boys too young for the army but with 5-10 years experience cowboying and quite a few of the older hands were too broke up to pass an army physical. This was a time and an area with lots of farms and small ranches; the people still lived on and made their living from the land. There were schools at places like Maryneal, Palava and Eskota – some of which today exist only in old timers memories – and help was available to gather a pasture, work calves or to do whatever needed doing horseback. It was a little harder to find help to build fence or drench sheep. It has been a long time but the men that I remember being at one or more workings on the gyp lease were Dad, Mr. Walter Boothe, Ray Boothe, Spot Hale, Alvin Estes, Walter Estes, Monk Hollowell, Whop Smith, Charlie Smith and Blunt Carson. At five years of age my first "cowboying job" was also on the gyp lease at a calf working. I was in charge of dragging up wood and tending the branding fire. I wasn't allowed to ride my own horse during the gather, too easy to get lost when the run started. Besides even the steady old horses that I got to ride would go to the sound of a cow popping brush like kids to the bell on an ice cream wagon and charge any hole in the brush big enough for them to fit through; anybody on their backs had to look out for his own self. I remember the sensation of riding behind Dad on cow chases with a saddle string clenched in each hand and my face buried in his back. The sudden jerks, swerves and jumps would put a carnival ride to shame and it was even more gut wrenching because I couldn't see them coming. Dads' old high cantle saddle and bat wing chaps protected my legs and his body kept most of the limb whips off me even when he was stretched out flat on the horses' neck so we would fit through a tight hole. I learned quickly to mimic every sway and bend that Dad made to keep him between the brush and me. The sounds and smells are still vivid; horses grunting, brush popping and men cussing overlaid with the smell of horse sweat, man sweat, dust and Lucky Strike tobacco. This was my introduction to the world of men and to the fact that there were some things that we didn't do and some things that we didn't talk about around the womenfolk. I knew that we cut the testicles off of the bull calves so that they wouldn't breed the heifers long before I knew why they would want to breed the heifers. It was hard dangerous work and some of the men were a little rough around the edges but the coarse language and violent horseplay stopped the moment a woman came into view. It was a time when right and wrong were still absolutes and everyone was expected to – and most did – live accordingly. Poor behavior occurred but it was not widely condoned or – as is too common today – celebrated. It was about this time too when Dad first impressed on me that both his and my main duty as men was to take care of and protect our womenfolk in every way. The political correctness police would have a hemorrhage today but it was heady stuff for a kid trying to learn to be a man.

Deep Sand and Mad Cows

THE ONLY CORRAL on the gyp lease was a bull wire pen maybe 100 feet square with a water trough on one side and a snubbing post in the middle. The cattle would be gathered and loose herded in the corner of the pasture that held this pen. Since there were cattle belonging to two different brands, a roper would ease through the herd until he paired up a cow and calf, rope the calf and drag it into the pen to the mugging crew where he would call out the cows' brand. The mugging crew threw the calf and held it on the ground so it could be vaccinated against blackleg, dehorned, branded and the bull calves castrated. It was my job to bring the right hot iron; either Diamond O or W D connected and take the iron back to the fire to re-heat after the calf was branded. All of the cows were horned and most of them were more than a little waspy so somebody opened the gate for the roper to drag in a calf and then shut it back to keep momma from coming in and expressing her displeasure at how her offspring was being treated. With two ropers coming and going, ever so often a cow would make it into the pen and proceed to run the mugging crews up on the fence until the ropers could haze her back outside. I suspect that sometimes when Whop Smith was on the gate the accident was kind of on purpose just to liven things up. The fence was six-foot bull wire with a board on top and another about three feet up from the ground. A grown man could step up on the first board and on up on top if momma was real serious but a three foot tall five year old had a problem. If somebody was close, I got snatched up and set on top of the fence, if not there was nothing to do but beat her to the water trough and dive in. You have no idea how long a cows tongue is and how loud she can bellow until you are eye level and two feet away from a really mad cow.

Since wormies (screwworm cases) were sometimes doctored and then held up and fed in the pen, the ground was churned up deep sand that was like running in glue. To this day I remember straining everything in me to stay ahead of one of those old biddies.

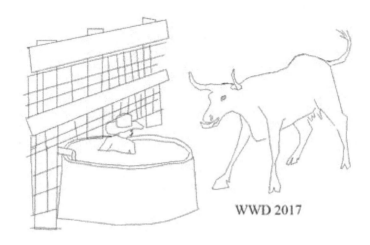

WWD 2017

Dad told me that if I was about to get caught, to just fall down flat on the ground and let her go over me. He promised that cattle would not step on me and while she might root me around with her nose and slobber all over me, she couldn't horn me if I stayed flat. I guess I believed him but I damn sure didn't want to put it to the test.

Many years later Mother told me how her Father had told her the same thing when she was about six. She never had the occasion to try the advice until after she and Dad were married. They bought a bull and hauled him to the home ranch at Decker in an old rattletrap trailer. As Dad opened the trailer gate, the bull lunged forward breaking through the trailer floor and injuring a leg. The wounded bull whirled back – looking to make someone pay for his pain – and cut Mother off from the trailer. She ran for the fence but was losing ground fast and about to be gored when she heard her Father say "fall flat Glynne Del, fall flat". She fell flat, the bull jumped over her and Dad was able to distract him until she could get to safety. Mother never doubted that her long dead Father had intervened to save her life.

Screwworms

THE SCREWWORM WAS – and in parts of South America and Africa still is – one of Gods' more unpleasant creatures. The adult female fly lays her eggs in open wounds on all kinds of animals where the eggs hatch and the resulting worms proceed to eat the host animal alive. Unlike other fly maggots (which only eat dead flesh and can actually be beneficial to the host animal) the screwworm eats only live flesh. Prior to screwworm eradication, wildlife experts say that, in the south, half or more of each year's fawn crop would be killed by screwworms. The adult flies lay eggs on the fresh navel wound and any calf born in the peak of screwworm season was almost certain to become infected. The mother cows, deer and other animals did their best to lick their babies clean but often they failed. Not only baby animals were at risk; an open wound of any kind, a thorn scratch or any break in the skin and all animals including humans could be infected. Ranchers spent a lot of time and money trying to protect their animals with only some very crude in-secticides to work with. The momma cows looked upon the medicine we put on their calves as the problem and proceeded to lick it off as soon as possible.

We tried all sort of recipes from coal tar to creosote to formaldehyde to try to keep the cows from licking the worm dope off the calves; the cows would grimace and slobber but they wouldn't quit licking until they got all that nasty stuff off their baby. I got an educa-tion on the degree of dedication this took when the big steer whose head wound I was doctoring – while straddling the chute over him – butted the bucket of worm dope into my crotch. I jumped down – shed my clothes in record time – jumped into the water trough and still wound up with a hell of a lot of blistered hide in some very uncomfortable places. Eradicating the screwworm in the U.S. and clear down to Panama was one of the few government programs ever that actually worked.

To this day if I get caught in a rain, my saddle smells like Smear 62 and EQ 335 and it has been over 45 years since I used either kind of worm dope to doctor a case of worms. About that long ago, I was doctoring wormies in the corral on the Oklahoma ranch with Dad and Edger McCleary when Bill, our neighbor to the east, drove up and fell in to help. We had a crowd pen and a squeeze chute so we could put each animal in the chute and treat its' wound without having to wrestle with them. I had a little wooden paddle that I used to dip the worm dope up out of the jar and smear it into the wound but Bill didn't bother with that; he used his fingers. Cow people don't tend to be too fastidious about cattle manure, blood and other bodily secretions. The old saw is you can't claim to be a cowboy till you've eaten five pounds of cow manure and drunk a quart of cow pee. So Bill using his bare fingers didn't turn any heads but several stomachs got a little queasy when Bill decided he needed a fresh chew of tobacco, slung off most of what was on his fingers and dug the old chew out of his jaw without even hunting a rag to wipe his hand.

Screwworms dictated everything we did when they were bad; we tried calving in the wintertime though this was hard on the cows and we worked calves on the hottest days of the year hoping the wounds would dry and form a crust before flies could lay eggs. Someone had to ride constantly from late April until a killing freeze doctoring wormies; a lot of the country was brush covered and infected animals tended to hide so we relied a lot on our sense smell to find them. I doubt that anyone who smelled a case of screwworms ever forgot the stench. If we missed an animal with an infected wound, the animal died a horrible death.

Sometime in the early 1960's I went with Sam Lambert to look at a ranch he was thinking of buying in southwest Colorado. That ranch was one of the roughest I have ever been on; the house was built on the most level spot I saw in a long day of riding and when they leveled the floor, they had room to park their vehicles underneath on the downhill side. The man who owned the ranch was originally from Snyder Texas and when we asked how they came to be there, he said "Screwworms, I left Snyder with a bunch of screwworms in a bottle and when I got to where nobody knew what they were, I bought a ranch." Anybody who ranched in the South when screwworms were bad would understand.

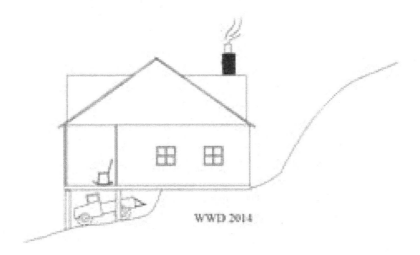

WWD 2014

The Real Professionals

A LOT HAS been written about the skill and nerve of the working cowboy but, to my mind, not near enough has been written about working ranch horses. The horses I am talking about are not the pampered celebrities you see helping rodeo cowboys catch and tie down calves in a few seconds. I am talking about the horses that go into the brush to catch and drive or drag out cattle that don't want to come. A lot of these horses are not much to look at and most of them are on the small side. Apt as not they will be barefooted, expected to make their living on grass alone and have little or no experience with a currycomb. Their pedigrees are seldom mentioned, even if they are known; they are valued not for who they are but for what they do. It is impossible to rein a horse on a course through really thick brush at a dead run after cattle. The horse has to pick his own path and want to catch the animal and the rider has to have sense enough to let him. A lot of these horses are cold jawed – the result of terrified cowboys sawing on the reins certain that they are about to run smack dab into that big mesquite when the horse has already picked the path he is going to take around that tree and the next three besides. The good ones decide that it is easier to just take the bit in their teeth and ignore the rider until it is time for him to do his part. This lack of worry about his rider is also evident in the size of the holes that a good brush horse picks; the criterion is "Is it wide enough to clear my chest and tall enough to clear the saddle horn?" You don't spend a lot of time sitting tall in the saddle when one of these ponies takes you on a cow chase. You are either stretched out flat on his neck or hanging off to one side far enough to give a Comanche warrior heart palpations. These horses look on their job as catching the cattle; it is not in their job description to worry about whether or not you are still aboard when they do. They do, however, expect you to do your job when the time comes. I have ridden more than one that would get you up for the second or even third loop but at some point most of them will say, "To hell with you Jack, if you can't catch it, then I'm not going to chase it." Not all horses have what it takes to be a good brush horse; not all have the desire and the heart to tolerate the pain it takes to get the job done. A common comment about a horse that didn't measure up was "That horse is just too thin skinned." The same comment can sometimes apply to cowboys. When you are going "hell bent for leather" over slick rock hills or popping branches as big as your arm off of mesquite trees, it is easy to feel the allure of a career selling used cars.

Nowhere was a good brush horse more valuable then when doctoring screwworm cases. When an animal is suffering, its inclination is to get off by its self and hide. This tendency is especially strong in sheep and goats; so much so that ranchers would put empty barrels and crates in out of the way places in the pasture and check these first when looking for worm cases. In rough, brushy pastures it is very hard to locate animals that are actively hiding. A good ranch horse would locate these animals by smell and go to them. I have seen, when the wind was right, horses go straight as a string to a worm case from a quarter mile away. It can be very useful but a good nose is not something normally associated with horses. The smell of a case of worms is powerful, so powerful that I hope I never smell it again.

Many a head of livestock has been spared a slow and painful death because ranch horses did their jobs. The good ones can be very good indeed; I have known horses that would bite a chunk out of a balky cow and kick hell out of a cow or bull that hooked at them toodle a baby calf along by pushing its butt with a lower lip. Occasionally you do find a horse that seems to hate cattle, biting or kicking anytime cattle are in reach. I have known several of these and every one of them had been spoiled by riders forcing them to crowd cattle in the pens. When a horse is forced to wade into cattle, it is very prone to injury to its' front knee joints and tries to protect itself by striking out at the cattle. Come to think of it, I know very few if any horse "faults" that are not caused by people.

It's a Cowboys Life

THE GYP LEASE had plenty of mesquite and rattlesnakes and if they could have sprouted would have had bumper crops of spurs, hats and ropes because lots of them were planted over the years. On one of the gathers, a bull came into the herd dragging a rope and so gaunt that he had obviously been hung up in the brush. Mr. Boothe stood all of his five and a half feet up in his stirrups and called out "Whose rope is that?", nobody said anything so again "Whose rope is that?", finally from across the herd came "That rope belongs to that bull, I give it to him three days ago." Mr. Boothe was a small mild mannered man who didn't come to the cattle business until he was full grown but he was pure cowman. When he was in his eighties, he worried his family sick by going out to the Boothe home ranch under Nine-mile Mountain to ride by himself. They had a pasture full of steady horses but he would catch a two year old to go to the pasture because "he needs the work." Mr. Boothe was in his sixties when he and Dad had the gyp lease and worked just as hard as the young men. People took falls and men and horses got stove up but no one was hurt badly. Dad told of once when he and Mr. Boothe were in a dead run on a cow chase and Mr. Boothes' horse fell throwing him forward like a canon shot. Just before he hit the ground Mr. Boothe ducked his head in a tumbling roll from his college days and rolled head over heels four or five times before coming to his feet unhurt.

Dad wasn't as lucky the day a mesquite snag came in under his chaps and over his boot top to bury up in the calf of his leg. He gritted his teeth and pulled out a piece an inch in diameter and twelve inches long and thought he had it all. Years later a dark shadow came up on his leg and x-rays showed that he had a piece at least as big as the one he pulled out still in his leg. Doctors were afraid removing it would cripple him so he lived with it the rest of his life. Getting perforated with thorns and cactus stickers is just part of a brush country cowboys' life but twelve inch thorns are a little over the average.

Sometimes getting bucked off or run over isn't the worst of it. Not long after Diann and I married, a cow butted me in the chest and separated my sternum for the second or third time. I have had a lot of things broken over the years but for sheer misery, I think a separated sternum takes the cake; a separated sternum makes broken ribs feel like something to look forward to. Anyway, I was lying on the bed breathing as shallowly and as infrequently as possible and doing my best not to move anything but my eyeballs and them slowly when Diann came in from town. After fussing over me a little, she said that she had run into our preacher at the grocery store and that he had enquired about my health. "I don't know what is wrong with that man, he went white as a sheet and scurried off when I told him that a cow hit you and separated your scrotum." I hadn't hurt at all compared to what that laughing fit felt like and to make it worse every time I got it under control, my brain would conjure up the expression on Preachers face and here it comes again.

Which Way is Up?

BETWEEN THE FLAT ground and the thick brush, the gyp lease was an easy place to get turned around if you couldn't see the sun. When I got in Boy Scouts, they told us if we were ever lost we could find our directions because the moss grows on the north side of trees. Problem is in west Texas moss doesn't grow on any side of trees. Anyway, just about everybody that rode on the gyp lease, sooner or later, got lost enough that they would have to ride until they hit a fence and follow it until they could get their bearings. One smooth cloudy day Mother brought dinner out to the crew and I was along with her for the ride. Dinner for those of you not west Texans is eaten close to noon not at suppertime. Winding through the brush on the faint little dirt road, we came around a bend and nearly caused a good cowhand to die of terminal embarrassment. Walter Estes was not fifty feet off the road trying to make his horse stand still enough that he could stand up in the saddle and hope to see something he could use to figure out where in the hell he was. He had made a run through the brush and lost not only the cow but his directions as well. From the look on his face I really believe Walter would have rather have been snake bit than to have a woman and kid catch him in that predicament.

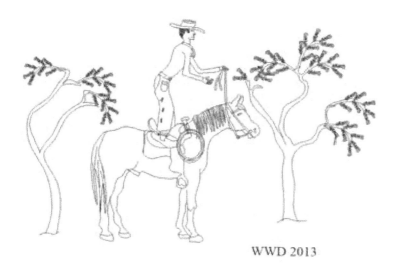

WWD 2013

It doesn't seem reasonable that a top hand like Walter could be lost fifty feet from a road but the road was just two wheel tracks and the brush was awful thick.

Wild Cows and Wild Cowboys

THE CATTLE ON the gyp lease were wild because of the way they were handled. They were normally penned only twice a year, in the late spring to work calves and in the fall to ship the calves to market. From April until the first killing frost someone had to ride almost continuously to find, rope and doctor screwworm cases. The only time those cattle saw a man horseback; he was trying to do something unpleasant to them so it was no wonder that they tried to get as far away as possible. Cattle respond to handling good or bad; show me a bunch of wild cattle and I will show you a bunch of wild cowboys. There are differences in temperament between breeds of cattle but most differences in behavior come from how the animals are handled.

Brahman cattle have a reputation for wildness and some live up to the billing but the gentlest set of cattle I have ever seen were purebred Brahman. I contend that Brahman cattle are smarter than your average cow and respond to handling more like horses; they have imagination, pride and self awareness. Mr. J.W. White, a registered Brahman breeder, out of Hearne Texas had a standing offer for years. Come to his place and point to one of his cows standing in the pasture; Mr. White would walk up to the cow, pet her, milk her, crawl under her belly and milk her on the off side. If she walked off before he got all this done, he would give her to you – the only requirement was that you then do the same with one of your cows. A lot of people, including dairymen, came to accept the challenge but they all turned crawdad and backed out before it was over. In 1960 I went to Mr. Whites' ranch to buy a bull and watched an amazing demonstration. Mr. White had forty or so cows with calves and a bull in a small pen. Several cows were in heat and the bull was working and so there was a lot of commotion in a confined area. Mr. White went into the pen, got down on his hands and knees and proceeded to crawl all through the pen going under cattle, scratching cows bellies and petting baby calves. Mr. White was not a young man and probably was getting pretty brittle but he believed that the cattle would look after him and he was right. Anytime you came to the White Ranch, you had to go up to the house and let Mrs. White serve ice cream. Mr. White called ice cream his "marketing plan" and said that fifty dollars worth of ice cream a year would sell all the cattle he wanted to sell. I ate the ice cream, bought a bull and felt like a member of the family before I left but Mr. White and his cattle were what sold the deal. The bull I bought had a registered name about a yard long that was soon reduced to "Joe"; Joe kept his easy going disposition all the years we owned him. At one time we had several hundred of his daughters in the cowherd – he regularly sired 80 – 90 calves a year – and while they were not as gentle as Mr. Whites' girls, I wasn't as good a cowman as Mr. White.

WWD 2014

Bunch Quitters

WHEN DAD AND Mr. Boothe gave up the gyp lease, cleaning the pasture became a major undertaking. They started with eight or ten hands and got most of the cattle in just a few days but there were twenty or so cattle that would not be driven out with the herd and learned to hide like deer. When anyone jumped one of these bunch quitters, he did his best to stay with it until they got to a place where he could swing a rope. When they caught one, they would tie it to a tree until they could come back with some help to lead and/or drag it out. One cloudy drizzly day Dad and Charlie Smith jumped a two-year-old heifer that they had run at three or four times without catching. Dad got separated and stopped to see if he could hear the chase. When he got quiet, he could hear Charlie hollering "Willis, ho Willis" way off in the distance. Dad got there as quick as he could to find Charlie, his horse and the heifer all completely run down but with the wet switch of the heifer's tail caught in the loop of

Charlie's' rope and his pony keeping a tight rope. Her outlaw days were over because like the song said, Charlie had "a rope in my hand and a cow by the tail".

They wound up roping and dragging out all of the bunch quitters one at a time, the last few Ray Boothe had to spot from the air in his Piper Cub airplane. He would find one hiding and then fly low and slow into the wind over the riders, cut his engine so they could hear, and holler down directions. He wouldn't be 100 feet in the air and no way that he could glide to a landing spot but his engine always restarted when it had to. Ray was an experienced pilot when the joined the Army Air Corps so they made him a flight instructor during World War II. This was pretty good duty but it got even better when they assigned him to Avenger Field, ten miles from his home in Sweetwater, to teach the young ladies of the Women's Army Air Corp to fly.

They tell a tale about another Nolan County airplane driving cowboy that turned out different. Jack Jones (or something like that) had spent three days with a big crew cleaning some rough canyon country of a bunch of big steers. The steers were Florida "brimmers" that weren't exactly gentle when they arrived in west Texas and after almost a year in the brush, their temperaments resembled those of the deer with which they shared the canyon breaks. It was a hell of a job but the crew finally got the cattle more or less together and out on the flats at the canyon mouth, from there it would be no problem to trail them to the pens. Just as they got the last cattle out of the canyon, Jack's son, who hadn't helped on the gather, came roaring in toward the herd about forty feet high in his airplane – scattering cattle, horses and cowboys and spooked every steer back into the rough country. They say that when Jack got his horse back under control; he sat there and cussed the kid – without repeating himself – for ten minutes straight.

The Dark Side of Cowboying

COWBOYING IS MORE than just riding and working cattle; the dark side of the profession that no one talks about is fencing and windmilling. Monk Hollowell worked for Dad for many years and was my boss when I got big enough to work. One of the summer projects that is still vivid in my mind is the time Monk and I rebuilt a mile of fence on the north side of the Decker ranch. We put in a cedar post every twelve feet and in the 440 three-foot deep postholes there were maybe a dozen that were dug totally in dirt. Most had three to five inches of soil over caliche, which is a not quite rock mixture of almost limestone and gypsum gravel with lots of limestone rocks mixed in. This is the material used to make all of the country roads in west Texas and has the property of setting up like concrete when it dries after being wet. A pair of standard wooden handled posthole diggers would just bounce when slammed down on caliche so we replaced the wood with steel pipe – this made the diggers four times as heavy so that they could sometimes penetrate a quarter or even a half-inch if slammed down hard enough. Where the diggers would work, the routine was to pick them up about eighteen inches and power them down as hard as possible, and then you rotated the diggers 90 degrees and did it again until you got enough loose material in the bottom of the hole to pick up by pinching together the blades of the diggers. Where the caliche was too compacted and when you hit solid rock, the diggers were abandoned in favor of a forty pound rock bar and a tin can. The rock bar was a steel bar about six feet long and an inch and a quarter thick with a long point forged on one end and a flattened chisel point on the other.

WWD 2014

To use this high tech equipment, you slammed the bar down where the post hole was to be and when enough chips were accumulated – or when you gave flat dab out lifting the bar – you got down and dipped out the rock chips with the tin can. It's not fair to say that we didn't have any high tech equipment; we had a tractor mounted posthole drill that Monk had modified to take a standard eight inch oil well drill bit. It spun plenty fast enough but was a little short on down pressure even when we rigged a weight boom and swung two old truck engine heads from it. We would start a hole with the rock bars then fill it with water and start the drill. On a good day and provided we kept the hole full of water, this rig would drill a rock hole in about two hours which was about the same rate as us human diggers. I hadn't thought about that rig in years but it taught me a valuable lesson one day when the tractor muffler got loose and fell off after several hours of running. It is not wise to pick up hot iron when you are wearing rubber-palmed gloves. Anyway, I was learning to build fence the right way from a master who tolerated no shoddy work or short cuts. I learned just what a perfectionist Monk was when we got ready to set the last brace in the fence. Where the last or gate post was to be fell in the middle of a flat rock about twenty feet in diameter. My suggestion that we move the gate post about ten feet east and make the gate wider was quickly vetoed and we spent two days chipping a four foot deep, sixteen inch diameter hole in solid rock. When it was finally finished, I commented that at least we would not need the brace post that we normally put six feet out from the corner post to prevent the end post from leaning when the strain of the stretched wires came on it. Monk looked at me like I had made an obscene comment in church and set me to pecking out the hole for the brace post. When this hole was at last done, I didn't even comment I just started pecking out the two foot by one foot by three foot deep hole that would hold the chunk of rock or "dead man" from which a doubled number nine galvanized wire would be run to the top of the brace post and twisted tight to make certain nothing moved. I feel certain that when archeologists discover those holes thousands of years from now, they will be taken as evidence of labors of devotion – sort of like the pyramids – to the god of some long forgotten religion.

Perhaps the funniest – if you were watching not doing – of Monks and my adventures had to do with windmilling. Much of west Texas is watered by windmills, which like all things mechanical must be serviced and repaired. Occasionally sucker rods break or pump leathers wear out and the pipe must be pulled out of the well so that repairs can be made. This can be hard, disagreeable work but is not really that big a deal. The big deal came when Monk and I had to climb the windmill tower and work on the mechanism thirty feet up in the air; I remembered it as sixty feet – maybe seventy – until I went back and checked. The problem was that Monk and I both were terrified of heights and it didn't help that the wind always blows in west Texas and the higher you go the harder it blows and the more the tower sways and creaks and moans. I am sure that a video of Monk and me both standing on the little two foot by two foot platform on top of a windmill tower trying to fix the broken tail control cable while dodging the wildly spinning sail and neither one of us willing to release the death grip he has with one hand on the tower so we could get it done would be amusing. It was not amusing at the time, with Monk telling me to "Give me the 9/16th wrench out of my pocket" and me reaching around his ample middle to try to fish the desired tool out of his overall pockets without sending both of us off the tower to eternity. It didn't help that his pockets held an amazing amount of tools; anytime Monk was doing mechanic work, the tools disappeared into his pockets at a rapid rate; two hours would empty the best stocked toolbox of all but rusty bolts and broken screwdrivers. I feel certain that every windmill tower I ever climbed has my handprints forever imbedded in its steel and Monk was much the same but with Monk there was never any question of not doing what needed to be done. It was suck it up and get it done whether it was climb the tower or get back on the horse that had just thrown you.

Monk put up with a lot trying to make a hand out of me and I like to think that some of his lessons stuck. Monk was the first person that got me to really look at cattle. Dad ran Hereford cattle and one Hereford looks a whole lot like the next one; they have been line bred for hundreds of years and are so close kin that they all have the same blood type but there are differences. One day Monk and I had sorted the calves off some cows and had one cow that we were going to put in the trailer and take to Dads' Fisher County place. Monk told me to go get the cows' calf out of the calf pen to put with her. I looked at that pen full of red white-faced calves that looked as much alike as peas in a pod and asked him "How the hell am I supposed to know which is her calf?" Monk snorted, walked over, pointed to a calf and said, "Open your eyes and look, it looks just like her." It didn't look just like her to me that day but I finally learned to actually see instead of to just look. He didn't tell it to me but a compliment that I prize highly came when – many years later, Monk told Diann – who was to be my wife – that I was "as good a hand with cattle as I have ever known."

Flying Cow Buyers

Just before Christmas 1970 my Father-in-law, Jeff Christian, asked if I would fly down to 7-11 Ranch out of Bourne Texas and show a potential cow buyer a set of half Santa Gertrudis half Red Angus cows that Louis Nagy had for sale. Jeff would normally have made the trip since 7-11 had been a client of his for years but he was tied up and couldn't get away when the rancher wanted to make the trip. I agreed to go and showed up at the ranch we were to take off from a little before daylight. The fellow wanting the cows was going to fly us down in his own plane; I had never met the man but Jeff assured me that he was a very experienced pilot. I helped the man push his little Air Coupe out of the barn and when we got it out into the light, it was obvious that regardless of his experience, he was flying a very experienced airplane. That little plane was covered in grime and oil streaks, had dents and dings all over it and while nothing fell off while we pushed it out, it looked very tired sitting on that dirt strip. Against my better judgment, I climbed in and strapped down as he started his take off routine, which consisted mostly of, "start damn it, start". When this didn't work, he climbed out and opened the engine cover and tinkered with something then went back into the barn and came out with a can of WD 40. He applied a liberal amount of WD 40 to whatever part was offending and then climbed back into the cockpit to try again. Still nothing so he climbed out, made another trip to the barn and came back with a two-pound hammer that he used to beat hell out of something in the engine compartment. I was clawing at my door latch while trying desperately to think of some excuse that would allow me to save face and still climb out and leave when the engine sputtered and the prop began turning with a pup-ata-pup-ata sound like it might be hitting on two cylinders. This distracted me long enough for him to do something with the controls that made the engine level out and before I could react, he had the engine revved up and we were rolling down the strip. Evidently the strip was pretty short because we had not much more than left the ground when he pulled the nose up in a steep banking climb and out the side window I saw some electric lines pass just a few feet beneath us. I guess I had lost those power lines in the oil streaks on the windshield and on reflection this was probably a good thing. Anyway we were flying, my pulse was down to no more than 150% of normal and the engine sounded pretty good so I stuck a cigarette in my mouth and was about to light it when he screamed, "Don't light it! For Gods' sake don't light that, I've got a bad gas leak!"

That trip to 7-11 and back was the longest 800 miles I ever made and to top it off, he didn't buy the cows.

Rattler Heaven

A MAJOR FEATURE of the gyp lease was the snakes, any time you got down you had better be watching and it wasn't the place to ride a horse that was scared of snakes. Sonny was just a short three-year-old when a rattler on the Gyp Lease bit him; for the rest of his life he was at war with the whole snake tribe and would stomp to death any snake he caught in the open. He grew into a huge horse and delighted in jumping into the air to land all four of his big feet on his enemy until there was nothing left but a greasy spot.

If you were on him at the time you took a jarring but that was better than making him mad by trying to ride him off before he was finished with the snake.

There were so many rattlesnakes that nobody tried to kill every one they saw, you wouldn't get anything else done; you learned to watch and just kind of go around them. At this time there were people that made a living catching rattlesnakes and selling them to anti-venom manufacturers. One of these men had been working the gyp lease and the adjoining Newman ranch and had a ten foot round water trough under a shade tree at the Newman pens with about a foot of snakes in it. Dad and Mr. Boothe had borrowed the Newman pens for a calf working and had gathered the cattle into a little trap next to the pens late one evening. We got there just after daylight ready to start work to find rattlesnakes everywhere. Someone had been poking at the trough full of snakes and left a stick slanting up to the lip of the trough. Every snake crawled out and there were snakes everywhere around those pens. Each fence post, broom weed and mesquite bush had at least one snake in its shade and you couldn't walk anywhere without setting snakes to singing. There was nothing to do but turn the cattle out and come back to try again after the snakes had scattered back into the brush.

Another story tells about the snake catcher that was bunking with the cowhands while he caught snakes on a big ranch just under the cap rock of the high plains. He was not real sociable and didn't have much to do with the hands so of course they had to devil him ever chance they got. One night the whole crew was playing cards in the bunkhouse when the snake man came in, pulled off his clothes and without speaking to anybody, crawled into his bed. His feet hadn't more than hit the bottom when he threw off the blankets and jumped clear out into the middle of the floor. The poker game was forgotten as the cowhands broke up whooping, laughing and hollering; they had caught a big rattler, sowed his mouth shut and tied him in the snake catchers' bed. The snake catcher didn't say a word; he just cut the snake loose from his bed, cut the stitches holding his mouth shut and tossed him into the middle of the card table. Story doesn't say but I bet those boys left the man alone.

Campus Cops and the
Baby Rattlers

IN 1960 KNOWING I was going home from Texas A&M College for the annual rattlesnake roundup at Sweetwater Texas, some of the wildlife management majors asked me to bring them some baby rattlers for a project that they had going. When I started back to school, I put thirty little rattlesnakes in a tow sack, tied it shut and put that sack in another, tied it shut and put it in the truck of my car. The wild lifers met me in the dorm parking lot and we drew quite a crowd as we fished the rattlers out of my sack and transferred them to three cages. We were getting crowded pretty good until somebody dropped a snake on the pavement and then we had a little more room. I had promised ten snakes to each of three guys and made sure I left with thirty snakes but when we counted them out, I only got there with twenty-seven. I looked good in my car, even took the back seat out but no snakes.

Several days passed without any sign of the missing snakes and I more or less forgot about them until one night two campus cops came to my dorm room to ask me if I owned a gray and white, 1956 Chevrolet car. They already knew it was my car from the parking sticker but asked because they wanted to search it. I said fine but what were they looking for? It seems that some tools had been stolen from a construction site and a beat up gray and white 1956 Chevy had been seen in the area. Dad had given me the car earlier that year when he got ready to buy a new one. To understand why a four-year-old car gets labeled "beat up" you need to know a little about Dad's driving habits. He operated on the theory that if he could go there horseback, then he should be able to go there in his car. The first time I saw this particular car, I was on top of Reese Canyon Mesa looking for wormy goats when I saw a strange car on the ranch road below. I rode out on a point and the driver evidently saw me because the car turned and started up the slope toward me. The car didn't come up a road – there wasn't one – it just came bouncing up over the rocks, washouts and shinnery brush, some-times spinning out and having to back up where the grade was too steep, until it got on top with me. It was Dad; he had picked up his new car and driven it out to the ranch. When he came through the cattle, he saw a new calf with a small case of screwworms in its' navel so he put it on the back seat floor board and came looking for me and the worm dope. We doctored the calf; he put it back in the car and took it back to the cows; that had to be the shortest-lived case of "new car smell" in history.

The well being of an automobile was of secondary importance compared to what he had going at the moment, such as chasing coyotes. One morning, he picked up Jim Wilson and me up from our stands to give us a ride back to the house after we had been deer hunting. I was in front and Jim was in the back seat when a coyote ran across the road in front of us. Dad took off through the brush after the coyote, swerving around the biggest trees and running over the rest and hollering for us to "shoot, shoot the S.O.B." while we bounced around in the car like dice in cup. We lost the coyote without ever firing a shot and when we got to camp Jim pulled me around behind the car to show me the 410 shotgun he'd had in case a turkey come by. The shotgun had been muzzle down in the back floorboard and had bounced hard enough sometime in the chase to bend the barrel. When Dad traded in a car, the dealer didn't even try to sell it in Sweetwater, it went straight to auction a long way from Sweetwater.

Anyway back to the campus cops, I went with them down to the car, opened it, and they began to dig through the stuff I had in the trunk. They were both waist deep in the truck when I remembered to tell them about the missing rattlesnakes. After that the search consisted of shining flashlights from about six feet away. They didn't find any stolen tools or any rattlesnakes and thanked me for my cooperation. One of them admired a horn from a big Angora Billy goat that was in the trunk, so I gave it to him to show them I had no hard feelings.

Good Snakes Bad Snakes

RATTLESNAKES WERE A real problem around Mother and Dads' first home on the Decker ranch; the house had a snake den under it. Rattlers were such regular visitors that Mother kept a hoe in the kitchen to kill the snakes that got in the house. She killed more than one by catching him going through a doorway and slamming the door on him; everybody had to be constantly on the lookout for snakes.

The bull snake is mortal enemy to rattlers so we would gather up every big bull snake we found and turn it loose around the headquarters. Dad told of finding a particularly big one when he was horseback a couple of miles from the house. He wanted to take that snake home but didn't have anything to put it in and knew he would lose it if he rode off to find a sack. The horse Dad was riding was a little bronky and he knew he would never be able to get back on him with the snake in his hands. Dad had

an idea; he tied the reins to the front foot of his horse –
there were no trees close bye – while he caught the snake
and then fed the snakes head between the two lower but-
tons of his shirt. Sure enough, all seven feet of that snake
crawled into his shirt and wrapped around his middle; as
skinny as Dad was then it probably made three wraps of
snake but the snake was out of sight and Dad untied his
horse. The pony couldn't see snake but he could damn
well smell him and he wanted no part of that snake stink
on his back. After three or four attempts, Dad cheeked
the horses' head around tight enough that he could get
on. The horse didn't like it and had a hump in his back
like a mountain top but Dad was sweet talking him and
petting him and finally he dropped the hump out of his
back and stepped off. He was moving but was still nervous and hunting boogers behind every bush. It looked
like they were going to make it when the snake made a
sudden break for freedom and stuck two feet of snake out
where horse could see it and the show was on. Dad pretty
quick forgot trying to hold on to snake since he had all
he could do to stay on his horse. It probably would have
worked out if snake hadn't draped his self around the
horses' neck on his way to the ground; that brought forth
some serious effort from the horse and Dad not only lost
his snake but had to walk home as well.

WWD 2013

Having bull snakes around helps with rattler problems; Joe Maddox recently sent me a series of photos showing a bull snake swallowing a rattler nearly as long as the bull snake. The main drawback to having the bull snakes around is that they have learned to vibrate their tails against the ground to imitate the sound a rattler makes. They won't hurt you but when one sounds off, it can damn sure make you hurt yourself. When we were rooming together in college, Norm Riggins, wired a rattlesnake rattle to an alarm clock clapper and used a pull string to set it to singing. For a while, every time I opened a draw or a closet, the rattlesnake booby trap would go off and I would have another set of heart palpitations. Intellectually, I knew that it wasn't a snake but that didn't keep me from jumping; it made my life miserable until it scared me one time too many and I stomped the damn thing to pieces. Snakes have an effect on people that has nothing to do with logic; it's like we are hard wired for fear and revulsion of snakes.

Monk Hollowell didn't like snakes even a little bit and was always real cautious about watching for them. One day, we were working on a propane storage tank that had a leaking valve. The tank was on skids so the bottom of the tank was about six inches off the ground and it was dark under there. Monk looked the area over real good; he even poked around with a stick before he squatted down to work on the problem. I was behind Monk, handing him tools in my usual role as swamper and go-for and had just stepped over to the tool box for something when, with an un-godly screech, Monk came flying bye me to land in a heap twelve feet from the tank. A big toad, whose home was under the tank, had enough of the disturbance and jumped out hitting Monk square in the face. It is amazing how far – given proper motivation – a middle aged fat man with an eighteen inch pipe wrench in each hand can jump backwards from a squatting position.

Saddle Shed Snake

WE TRIED TO keep bull snakes around the headquarters and for several years a nice sized one lived in the saddle shed; while it was there we had no trouble with rattlers or rats taking up residence. Most times when you opened the door, he would crawl off out of sight but if he was startled, he could make a sound by vibrating his tail against the ground that was close enough to a rattlers' song to make you wet yourself. This was particularly true when the door blew shut and the shed went dark as the inside of a black cat. I opened the saddle-shed door one cool day to find all six feet of Mr. Bull Snake stretched out right inside the door. The fellow with me that day was one of those people terrified of snakes; bull snakes, garters snakes, or rattlers, big or little, were all the same to Don and he wanted nothing to do with any of them. I knew how scared he was of snakes but that devil on my shoulder made me reach down, scoop up the snake then whirl around and pitch it so that it hit Don right in the face where it promptly coiled around his neck. Don went running backwards across the horse lot making a high-pitched squealing sort of noise while clawing at the snake with one hand and at the pistol he was wearing with the other hand but he wasn't making much progress with either hand; he couldn't leave the snake alone long enough to get the gun out. He ran backwards all the way across the lot finally hitting the board fence of the crowd chute which knocked him down and the snake off. Don was sitting flat on the ground watching the snake crawl away and I was laughing so hard I couldn't get my breath. Between fits of laughter, I told Don, "It's a good thing you couldn't get that gun out, you would have shot yourself for sure trying to shoot the snake." He looked up at me and dead serious said, "I wasn't trying to kill the snake, I figured I was dead anyway and I was going to shoot the son-of-a-bitch that threw the snake on me." Looking at his face cured my laughing fit and I didn't play any more snake jokes on Don.

When you live in a really snaky country, you learn to watch for snakes just like a city dweller learns to watch for traffic; you also tend to get a little blasé about them. I was delivering a tractor to one of Dads' customers up in Fisher County when I saw a good example. I had unloaded the tractor and the farmer and I were standing by the truck visiting when I saw three little kids coming down the dirt road towards us. The oldest boy was maybe ten; his brother about eight and little sister looked about six. They were all barefooted and as they got closer, I could see that the oldest boy was dragging something that he had tied to a stick over his shoulder. Little sister ran ahead and came up hollering "Daddy come look, we got a big one today." The boys came around the truck and I could see that the "big one" was a rattlesnake almost six feet long. The farmer said "Yep, that's a big one alright, don't you kids leave it in the yard to make a stink." And he went back to visiting. Quite a difference from the Pennsylvania State cop who showed me a little three button snake rattle and said "It took four rounds from my 357 Magnum to kill this thing." I didn't tell him but if you want to kill snakes with a pistol, load a 22 with rat shot. From eight feet one shot in the head will chill the biggest rattler.

Dad had a little place just a few miles from where the kids dragged up the snake and in the late 1950s an oil company drilled on it what we hoped would be an oil well. The location was right next to a rocky bluff that had several snake dens in it that were always good for some snakes when we were hunting. The crews killed several while they were making the location and getting the rig up. It was early spring and most snakes were still staying close to their winter dens, though they would venture out during warm days. They were not a major problem around the rig until it warmed up and drilling started. The roughneck on evening tour (tower in west Texas) whose job it was to catch drill-cutting samples was the first to see that they had a problem. He took a flashlight to catch the last sample of his tour and when he got back to the doghouse, he was white as a sheet and told the driller, "I am not going back out there in the dark, there are rattlesnakes everywhere!" Whether it was the vibration from the drilling or just that the rig was located in the path rattlers took leaving the dens, there were so many snakes around the rig that the crews worked only during daylight hours until they finished the hole. The hole turned out to be dry anyway.

When Diann was a little girl, my father-in-law managed the La Perla Ranch on the Rio Grande. One of her most vivid memories from this time is sitting on her horse Liberty and watching Mexican vaqueros make and use a horsehair noose to snare big rattlesnakes. They would put a horsehair noose on a stick and tease the rattler until it struck so they get the loop in its mouth. If it moved, those boys would figure out a way to rope it. About the only animal that I have never heard of anyone successfully roping is the armadillo; I have tried and seen other people try but it is just like trying to rope a basketball.

Dumb Animals?

I AM SURPRISED how many people even those that work with animals subscribe to the notion that animals are dumb. Nearly every animal I ever ran across knew everything it needed to know about being its kind of animal; that is not something you can say about most people.

In 1953 Dad gave me a three year old line back dun – what the Mexicans call a bayo coyote – named Monkey, he and I would do a lot of growing up together before he died of infectious encephalitis in 1960. Anyway, I hauled Monkey out to the Decker ranch and turned him out with the saddle horses. Being young and stout and full of vinegar, Monkey immediately challenged the two old saddle horses that were standing in the lot where I turned him loose. Red, the younger of the two at about twenty, squealed and snapped back when Monkey bit at him. Grayman, who was about twenty-seven and frail, made no attempt to fight but instead went out through the gate in a shambling run into the horse trap with Monkey snapping at his butt in close pursuit. I was squalling at Monkey and trying to catch up to protect the old horse when Grayman went over a low terrace and suddenly stopped with his front feet lower than his rear feet. Monkey came charging over the terrace with fire in his eye and Grayman timed it perfectly, kicking with both hind feet, he caught monkey under the chin with one hoof and in the center of the chest with the other. Monkey went down like he had been pole axed and didn't even twitch; I thought sure that I had just lost my horse. By the time I got there Monkey was groaning and rolling around and finally he staggered to his feet and stood there spraddle-legged and wobbly. Mean time Grayman was standing very nonchalantly with his rump to Monkey munching on some dry weeds like they were good. When Monkey turned and walked off, Grayman stretched out, took a long satisfying piss and calmly walked back into the pen to stand nose to tail with Red so they could switch the flies off each other's faces and doze. I never saw Monkey make another move toward Grayman and nobody can tell me that the old horse didn't know exactly what he was doing when he laid his ambush.

One time, years ago when I was still dumb enough to be calving in February, Homer Gilbert and I pulled into a pasture of calving cows with a load of hay. It had rained turning to sleet in the night and the cattle were bunched waiting at the gate. As we pulled in a cow lying down on the far side of the pasture raised her head and bawled; we threw the hay off as fast as we could and I left Homer pulling the wires off the bales and went to check on the down cow. The cow was lying in a drainage ditch with two feet of ice-cold water up to her shoulder and using her back to keep her newborn calf from sliding down the steep muddy bank into the water. I grabbed the calf, pulled it back up the bank and carried it to a level spot on some grass. The cow stood up when I took the calf and followed us to start licking her baby as soon as I laid it down. She had done the one thing that she could do to save her calf from drowning and that took reasoning power. She had done her job with a lot more intelligence than I did mine when I made her calve in the wintertime. I went back and got her a half a bale of alfalfa to eat all by her-self.

I topped a ridge on the Decker Ranch one day and saw, down below me, a whitetail doe with a wobbly brand new fawn following her. As I watched, the doe took the fawn into a chittamwood thicket to lay it down. The doe came out of the thicket and started off at ninety degrees from the way she had come and was soon out of my sight in the brush. I was about to ride on when I caught movement out of the corner of my eye and turned to see a fox trailing the doe and fawn. I was about to intervene when suddenly mama deer was all over that fox like ugly on an ape. She had circled back to check her back trail and caught Mr. Fox in the act. I had never seen a doe fight anything except play butting and front feet sparring with other does. She made no attempt to butt the fox but rather used her front feet like Sugar Ray Robinson uses his hands. She would slap that fox and send him rolling and be on him before he could get up to slap him again. He finally managed to break and run and went out of sight with her right on his tail. I didn't see the last of the drama but I bet Mr. Fox lost all interest in having venison for supper.

Not so Dumb Animals

D AD AND EDGER McCleary got in the hog business together soon after Dad bought the Oklahoma ranch.
They had a whole mess of big Duroc sows in a pasture
that fronted on Red River and they were feeding them
ear corn to supplement the forage they were getting. I
was feeding the sows one hot day and noticed one sow
wallow the corn around until she got two ears sideways
in her mouth and then run off towards the river. The
other sows were busy chowing down right where I threw
the corn out when I looked up to see the sow come back
and get two more ears and go back to the river. I followed
when I got through feeding and found a very intelligent
lady pig. While her sisters rooted around in the hot sun,
she was lying in the shade of a tree at the edge of the
river with cool water half way up her side and even had
a little shelf to hold her corn as she enjoyed her meal in
comfort.

About 1984 Dad bought some very good but old Santa Gertrudis cows of Maltsberger breeding and took them to the Decker Ranch hoping to get a calf crop or two from these grand old ladies. As he drove into their pasture one day, a cow bawled from the brush down on the canyon floor. He drove towards the sound and met a tight-bagged cow coming toward him; as soon as she saw him, she turned and went back into the brush. Dad followed and found a new born calf that had been licked off but was gaunt and obliviously hadn't nursed. Dad was a little dubious about picking up the calf, most of those cows were "good mommas", but she didn't threaten him when he picked up the calf so he carried it back to his truck with the cow right behind murmuring to her calf. He put the calf in the back of his Travel All and was afraid the cow would not follow since she couldn't see the calf but when he started off, she followed like she was on a lead rope the two miles to the pens and right into the pens. Dad put the calf down next to the squeeze chute and went back to put the cow down the chute so that he could milk her to get the milk flowing and the calf could nurse. Problem was the cow refused to enter the chute; she didn't fight or get upset she just refused to enter the chute. Dad was in the crowd pen with the cow and she didn't threaten him even when he pushed on her and twisted her tail, she just refused to go into the chute. Getting a calf to nurse on its' own when it has missed what should have been its' first meal within a couple of hours of birth can sometimes be a long back breaking process. Dad didn't want to get the cow upset because he might have to put her in the chute to nurse the calf twice a day for four or five days. The cow was raised in the brush country of south Texas, horned, weighted about 1500 pounds, and her only experience with men in pens was that's where they take you to hurt you. In the middle of the crowd pen, Dad started talking to the cow, petting her and finally eased a hand down and took hold of one of those swollen teats. He expected her to kick or at least shy away from him but she stood still as a stature while he massaged the teat, expelling the plug and starting the milk flowing. He brought the calf into the pen and holding it up to the teat finally got it to take hold and nurse. Dad fed and watered the cow and left her and the calf in the pen. Next morning he went through the whole process again except the calf was a little quicker to take hold and he didn't have to hold it up to the teat for as long. This went on for three days with Dad having to get the calf up and put him on the teat twice a day. The calf wouldn't nurse unless Dad was there; it associated him with food and wouldn't try unless he was holding him. The cow through all of this was a perfect lady; she stood stock-still and never once threatened Dad or kicked. The morning of the fourth day, Dad walked into the pen and the cow charged him and knocked him down then stood over her calf shaking her head and pawing dirt. The calf had learned to grab a teat and nurse by its self and she didn't need Dad anymore.

WWD 2017

My horse Monkey and I did our growing up together and there was a time or two when it didn't look like either of us would make it. We did OK as long as we stuck with everyday cow work with the wrecks being just the ordinary things that happen in that kind of work; it was when we got away from work that we got in big trouble. One such ordinary wreck was the time I roped a wormy calf just as it got to a patch of tall broom weeds; the calf ran into the tall weeds and neither it nor I saw the big cholla cactus until first the calf and then Monkey ran over it. The cholla is called the jumping cactus because its limbs grow under tension so that when anything touches it, the limbs snap forward driving the two-inch spines into man or beast. To top it off the spines are barbed so they are hell to pull out and are poisoned to increase the pain. That poor calf ran right into the cactus and had spines in his face, chest, legs, and all along his belly. Monkey had some spines in his legs and chest but the real damage was limbs of cholla, each with dozens of spines, stuck in his sheath and between his back legs. Monkey stood stock-still but quivering with his legs spread just as wide as they would go and sweat running off him like we had run five miles. The calf was bawling in pain and thrashing making his situation worse so I started on him. I drug him away from the cactus limbs that were scattered all over the ground, tied him down and started pulling spines with the pair of wire pliers that I luckily had in my saddle pocket. The limbs of a cholla are very brittle and about half the time when I pulled a limb off the calf, I wound up with part of it stuck in me. It took what seemed like forever but I finally got all the spines that I could find out, doctored the screwworm wound and turned the calf loose. Poor Monkey had never moved but was in terrible pain and I wondered if he would let me pull the spines without throwing a fit. I started on spines away from his hind feet but he never moved a muscle even when I was under his belly pulling spines out of his sheath and from the crease between his hind legs. He would moan a little when I pulled on a spine buried in a tender spot but never moved until I was through and led him forward.

I had a similar thing happen once when I jumped a horse off a creek bank and landed right in the middle of a tangle of barbed wire that had washed down the creek. Major, the horse I was riding, had once been badly cut on wire and was terrified of wire of all kinds; a piece of bailing wire lying on the ground would send him shying off in panic. When I realized what had happened, I jumped off and grabbed his head fully expecting him to throw a fit and cut off all four legs but he just stood there trembling with barbed wire on all of his legs. I was by myself with no place to tie the horse and no pliers to cut the wire away. The only thing I could do was start working one leg at a time getting it where I could lift the leg out of the wire tangle. As careful as I could be, I cut Major several times in the process of getting the wire off. Major was still trembling but as I cleared a leg and put it down, he never moved except when I asked him to lift a leg. I finally got him clear with only some minor scratches but when I tried to get him to pull the tangle out of the weeds so I could dispose of it, he refused to turn his back on the wire even at the end of a rope. There is no way anyone can convince me that both of those horses didn't know that I was trying to help and that their only option was to trust me.

A Really Dumb Animal

As I HAVE said Monkey and I were real lucky to survive each other; best example of this was the time I decided to teach him to let me shoot off of his back so I wouldn't have to get off every time I wanted to kill a rattlesnake. Really there were two big flaws in this plan; Monkey didn't like it a damn bit, even though I was careful not to shoot close to his ears, and also it assumed that I could hit a rattlesnake from the saddle. Anyway, I started by shooting from the ground where I could hold Monkey and calm him after each shot. He wasn't crazy about the deal but after a few shots, always with me between him and the pistol, he got to where he didn't flinch or try to jerk away when I shot so I decided it was time to try it from the saddle. The first shot startled him so that he shied sideways but I petted him and sweet-talked him until he settled down. The second shot made him mad and he jerked his head down and tried to pitch. I pulled his head back up and got him under control but he still had a hump in his back and if I'd had any sense I could have told that he'd had just about all the foolishness he was going to tolerate. The third shot was the deal breaker, when it went off Monkey lunged forward and turned it on. He had pitched with me several times and I was of the opinion that I could ride the best he could do, but the truth was he had never before been this motivated. He got his head completely away from me and was bucking harder than I thought he could and I still had the pistol in my hand. If I had been alone, I probably would have thrown the gun down – where it undoubtedly would have gone off and shot me – and used the free hand to get hold of something to try to stay in the saddle but Don Bryan was with me and I couldn't bring myself to let anyone see me cry "Uncle" like that. Monkey had been bucking straight away but now sucked back through himself and whirled back the way we had come. I made the turn but was getting awfully loose in the saddle when Monkey bucked into Don's horse and knocked my right foot out of the stirrup.

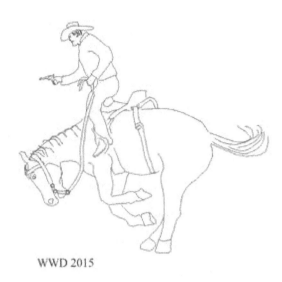

WWD 2015

That was it, I made a couple of more jumps but then his butt coming up caught mine coming down and I hit the ground. Or rather my shoulders hit the ground because I had stuck my left foot through the stirrup and I was hung up and Monkey was running. I remember being completely clear headed, not addled like you normally are when you hit the ground hard, and thinking that I needed to get loose before Monkey got to the brush and bashed me against a tree. I still had the pistol in my hand and the thought crossed my mind that I could shoot the horse but I was rational enough to know that even if the body shot eventually killed him, he would drag me to death before he died.

Don was in hot pursuit, trying to get hold of Monkey but I didn't know it at the time. Evidently me bouncing along behind him didn't suit Monkey because after about a hundred yards, he suddenly stuck his front feet in the ground and kicked me with both hind feet. That was the first and only time getting kicked by a horse felt good because he kicked me loose; my boot stayed in the stirrup but I was loose. Don got there about that time and Monkey stopped to see if the damn fool was going to get up and pester him some more. First thing I did after getting stood up and deciding that nothing important was broke was to put the pistol in my holster and buckle the hold down strap, enough was enough even for a dumb kid. I clawed up on Monkey and we went back to the pens like nothing had happened except that I was pretty sure my left leg was six inches longer than my right. When I got home I had to admit to bucking down but didn't feel the need to tell my folks the whole story. I was supposed to take a girl to a dance that night but by the time I got a shower, I was so stiff and sore that I decided to call and beg off going. When Mother heard this she showed a full measure of material compassion, "It's your own fault that you are sore, that girl has been expecting to go to the dance and she is going. Get dressed and go pick her up." I

went but that night Sweet Sue had to put up with dancing about on a par with my bronc riding.

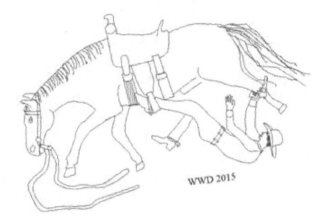

WWD 2015

Pet Coons

WHEN OUR GIRLS were little, I brought home a little female raccoon kitten from a nest under a hay bale. Her eyes were still closed but Diann quickly had her nursing from a doll bottle and before long eating Gerber's baby cereal. All was well until she crawled under my rocking chair as I rocked forward and mashed her head. When she squealed I snatched her up and was horrified to see that her head was flatted and one eye was protruding. Not wanting the girls to see, I took the coon outside expecting to have to put her out of her misery. As I carried her out, I very gently pressed on her skull and was amazed when it popped back into shape and the eye returned to normal position. I still expected the little coon to die but she never even missed a meal and was soon running all over earning her name Damn Coon or D.C. for short. As long as she was with us though, she would periodically get headaches and go, with one eye closed, to Diann who would give her half a baby aspirin and relief.

We soon learned that raising a baby coon was almost as much trouble as raising a human baby. Mama coons have to teach their babies everything, even how to climb, which we learned when D.C. climbed a tree in the front yard but fell out and broke a hind leg. We got the leg set and a wire frame splint applied and she was soon romping around on three legs while dragging the fourth. D.C. lived in the house but was housebroke and asked to go out when necessary just like a dog. The first time she asked to go out after getting her leg splinted, I followed because I was worried about her ability to manage with the splinted leg. She hobbled around the corner of the house and I followed, peaking around the corner only to get a sound cussing in coon talk making it plain that I was invading her privacy and to go the hell away. The leg healed and D.C. seemed to be good as new but the set was not quite right and the affected foot turned out just enough to give her a distinctive track.

We were not quite through with climbing adventures though as I learned when I came home to find Diann and the girls fit to be tied and D.C. sixty feet up in the big pecan tree at the edge of our yard. I tried to tell them that she would come down when she got hungry but all four of them jumped on me saying that she couldn't get down and that I had to do something or D.C. would die. There was no way that I could climb as high as the coon; the limbs wouldn't hold my weight, besides I was terrified of heights and wouldn't go that high even to keep my females from thinking me a wimp. After vetoing calling a ladder truck from forty miles away or hiring a helicopter, I got my bow and shot an arrow with a fishing line attached over a limb ten feet above the coon. Someone had to be watching over me because not only did I not put the arrow through the coon, but also my first shot went over the only limb that would let me pull the basket up to where D.C. could get in it. I tied a heavier line to the fishing line, pulled it up over the limb and used this line to pull up a basket with some sliced apple in it. I still had to climb to get to where I could pull the basket up to the limb D.C. was on but only about twenty feet high, which turned into fifty feet when I looked down. Anyway, I pulled the basket up to D.C. and all my females and I started begging her to "Get in the basket D. C., get in." D. C. kept up a steady stream of coon cussing as if I were to blame for her troubles but finally climbed into the basket and I lowered her down to me. When she reached me, she jumped out of the basket and onto my shoulder and when I reached up to put her back in the basket; she bit hell out of me. She would not get back in the basket so I climbed down with a coon on first one then the other shoulder except when she was on my head.

My Mother-in-law, Katty, was very strict about, "No animals in my house". So Diann and I were a little worried when we needed to ask her to keep our little girls and D.C. for a few days while we took a trip. We got back two days later and went to collect the girls' right after lunch. We quickly saw that our worry was not valid when we found all four little girls – counting the coon – conked out together for a nap on Kattys' bed.

D.C. quickly became part of the family, accepted by people, dogs and horses; the tomcat never did get to where he liked her but he was smart enough not to cross her. She slept with Diann and me; in the bookcase at the head of the bed when it was hot and under the covers at our feet when it was cold. D.C. was our alarm clock, she would start moving around when it was time to get up and if this didn't work, she would crawl up, put the end of her nose on the end of my nose and breathe on me while feeling my face with busy little hands. If this didn't work, she would stick a finger in your nose or ear and then you would get up.

Her habit of sleeping in our bed nearly caused us to lose a friend to heart attack. We had done an unbelievably dumb thing by having all three of the girls tonsils taken out at the same time; our thinking was, why drive back and forth the fifty miles to the hospital three times when we could get it all done at once. We finally got home from the hospital after twice as long as expected and after having to take Kelly back to surgery twice but all three of the girls felt bad and Diann's' Mother, Katty insisted that she come home with us to help, even though her friend Alva was there visiting. We put Katty and Alva in our bedroom as we sat up with the little girls and took turns napping on a cot in the girls' room. The girls were all feverish and uncomfortable so Katty sent Alva on to bed and the rest of us sat with the girls. Not long after Alva went to bed, we heard a scream and "Katherine George, Katherine George! There is something in this bed with me!" We all went charging back, turned on the lights and found Alva standing straight up in the middle of the bed in her nightgown and a very frightened little coon cowering in the bookcase. We had forgotten to tell Alva about D.C. Alva had gotten in bed, gone sound asleep and woke up to feel little hands feeling her face. It was a tossup who was more scared Alva or D.C.

D.C. was always free to come and go as she pleased and as she matured, she began to spend the occasional night out until one time she didn't come back. All four of my girls were frantic and insisted that she was lost and that I should go look for her. I had just about convinced them that she had found some coon friends to be with when she came dragging in looking like she had been on a weeklong drunk. She was hungry and completely out of character for her, dirty; she gobbled down the food the girls fixed for her and curled up in a corner to sleep for twelve hours. She left the next night and never came back into the house. After she had been gone for several days, I found tracks in the sandy road by our house; a small coon with a turned out hind foot and a big coon had come up the road from the river to our house and had spent some time milling around at the edge of the yard before going back toward the river. Later I saw D.C. at night out in the pasture; I drove up on a mama coon that I thought was D.C. and three kittens. She took the kittens up a tree and would come about half down and talk to me when I called but she would not let me touch her.

Kid Dogs are Special

OVER THE YEARS we have had some really special dogs; I guess when you think about it, all dogs are special. My first dog was Pooch; who was a Rat Terrier that thought he was a Bull Mastiff. Pooch probably weighted maybe six or eight pounds soaking wet but as far as he was concerned, he was as big as any dog. Actually Pooch was my Dads' dog but when I got to be about four, they both pretended that Pooch was my dog. Before I got mobile, Pooch made every step that Dad made. Dad raised what he called bundle feed to feed the horses and for emergency feed for the cattle. The standing feed was cut with a broadcast binder which cut the plants off at ground level and tied them in bundles and dropped the bundles out on the ground. Since the plants were cut green the bundles had to be stood up on end and leaned together in stacks called "shocks" to dry. The drying process normally took several days after which the bundles would be loaded on to a wagon and taken to the "stack lot" where they were stored in big stacks shaped to shed water. Hot summer sun will kill rattlesnakes that stay in it too long so, with the feed cut, the snakes that had come into the field to catch mice and birds crawled under the bundles to get out of the sun. When Dad was shocking bundles or when he was hauling in the shocks, Pooch was in charge of rattlesnake security. He would check each bundle or shock before Dad got to it and kill any rattler that he found. Dad said that more than once he had seen the little dog kill 5-6 snakes in one day. Pooch would tease the snake until it struck at him then grab the snake just behind its head and shake it to death. The rattlers were fast but Pooch was faster and he never got bitten.

By the time I was about four, Pooch and I were a team; one of our favorite games was where I moved boards and he caught the rats and mice that scurried out. One afternoon we began to find all kinds of baby mice in nests that I uncovered and I began to rescue them and put them in my cap. When the cap was full, I decided to take them to show Momma. Mother had a bunch of ladies playing bridge and visiting; I had already been banished outside but I was sure that the ladies would like to see my baby mice so I walked in and dumped my cap full of hairless baby mice in the middle of the card table. Pooch of course went with me, both of us proud of our accomplishment but when the screaming started, Pooch sold out and left me to gather up the mice, under strict orders and dire threats and take them down and throw them to the chickens all by myself. I didn't know that my Momma could be so mean.

Pooch and I were out in the backyard one day when a big German Sheppard had the audacity to not only come into our yard but to stop and heist his leg on the gate post. Unlike most little dogs, Pooch never did bark much and I don't remember him making a sound of any kind as he hit the big dog in a dead run. I was terrified that my dog was about to get eaten alive but Pooch handled the dog just like he handled snakes. He teased until the big dog lunged at him and then jumped aside to bite ears, nose or whatever was exposed. I was squalling and chunking rocks and Pooch was dancing in and out like Cassius Clay when he saw his chance and grabbed the Sheppard's' entire right ear in his mouth and showered down on it. The Sheppard squalled and yelped and went out of sight down the road with Pooch hanging on his ear. I was forbidden from leaving the yard but this was an emergency and I followed them as fast as I could run.

Turned out alright, I met Pooch coming back looking quite pleased with himself and we made it back to the yard without Momma knowing we were gone. That night I told Dad the whole story just like it happened but I don't think that he fully understood just how big the other dog was and how skilled and brave Pooch and I were in running him off.

WWD 2012

Not long after this I came running into the house to tell Mother that a horse ran through our yard dragging a man. She looked outside and told me to go play and to stop making up tales. When Dad came home, I overheard him telling Mother that a neighbor man had bucked off his horse and been dragged to death.

One of Jeff's clients gave our little girls a Labrador retriever that they named Kona for the Hawaiian island where she was born. She was soon established as "one of the girls" even when she lapsed and chewed the head off of one doll and an arm off of another; she stayed right with the girls and was very protective of them. I found out how protective when I fussed at Kelly and Quinn for some misdeed and Kona came to get between me and the two miscreants and look up at me and whine while wagging her tail. If she had been able to talk, she could have not made it any clearer that the girls were sorry and would not be bad anymore. She was wrong about that of course but would always take up for her girls; if I threatened to swat one of them Kona would take my arm in her mouth, not hard but business like, and whine, "Please don't do that." until she sensed that the threat was over.

The first dog the girls had was before we moved to the ranch; Bowser was a chow cross stray that showed up at Grandmother Kattys house and was immediately adopted by the girls. Bowser was pretty scruffy looking and from the scars and bitten ears had lived a hard life. He earned his place in the family though when Katty looked out the window to see him backing up with a mouth full of diaper dragging

Quinn back from the highway as she screamed bloody murder and tried to get to the forbidden road. Bowser moved with us to the ranch but would never come into the house. Soon after we moved in, it turned bitter cold and I had not yet built Bowser a dog house; Bowser was lying on the cold concrete in the carport when Diann physically dragged him into the house. She fixed him a bed in our bedroom where he lay down but sometime in the night, he decided to join us in our bed; sharing your bed with eighty pounds of wet dog is not fun but thankfully Bowser soon preferred his new bed in the carport. We all went into mourning when Bowser disappeared.

When our girls were still little, my older sister, Cissy, gave us a white German Sheppard female and we raised a litter of pups. We wound up with two male pups, Sancho and Teton that seemed to know from day one that their job was to take care of the girls. They made every step the girls did and the only things they were afraid of were Whiskers (the toy poodle) and Ruidoso (the duck). Whiskers weighted maybe 5 or 6 pounds but he got the Indian sign on Sancho and Teton when they were puppies and he kept it even when they weighed 100 pounds apiece; they did what he said or he jumped right in the middle of them like a little buzz saw. Ruidoso (she grew up with dogs and thought she was

Sancho and Tetons mother) would groom the boys and fuss at them like a fish wife when they came in muddy and full of cockleburs. They whined when she pulled their hair getting burrs out but cowered down and took it until she was through. The boys and Whiskers spent a lot of time hunting when the girls were in school and Whiskers would drag out anything that the boys ran into a hole; I have seen him come backing out of a hole dragging a full grown possum that weighed a lot more than he did. Hunting was fun but their job was taking care of the girls and nothing interfered with that; their efforts were not always appreciated (like when they tried to herd the girls out of the water and back to the bank when they were swimming). They seldom barked or growled but would always be between Diann and the girls and any stranger. One campaigning politician made the mistake of jumping over the fence too close to where Diann and the girls were picking up pecans; in truth, he sort of clambered over the first time but he jumped it easily going back. I could feel better about leaving Diann and the girls when the boys were there.

Coming to Oklahoma

WHEN I MOVED to the Oklahoma ranch, I had a German Sheppard pup named Sancho and a beagle pup named Bo; the three of us and Mrs. Cat – who adopted us – batched in a little cabin right on Red River. There were three miles of river bottom mud road out to the County dirt and gravel road and there were seven barbed wire gap gates across the mud road; when it was wet, I left my car at the ranch shop on the County road and went back and forth either in a 4-wheel drive jeep or horseback. Even this was a big improvement; when Dad bought the ranch in 1950, the closest all weather road at that time ended at Bennington eleven miles north of my cabin. We didn't get much company and the first cattle Dad brought to the place were unloaded at Bennington and driven to the ranch.

The cabin on Red River was built as a beer joint; Three miles deep in the river bottom timber on a dead end road would not seem to be a promising location for a tavern but it actually was a going concern. Texas across the river was dry for miles in all directions; people would come to the river bank on the Texas side, honk and hold up one of several premade signs and the man running the joint would put a case of Budweiser, Lone Star or whatever in a boat and take it across the river. It seems that Oklahoma owns the Red River to the high water mark on the south side; as long as the customer took the beer out of the boat, the deal was legal. Aside from his drive-in and boat-in business, the proprietor did a good weekend business with regulars that would come – good weather or bad – on Friday evening and stay until they ran out of money or Monday morning, whichever came first. It was not what would commonly be called a genteel establishment. On Sunday mornings there might be ten or fifteen people passed out drunk under the trees that surrounded the place. Tales were told (not where he could hear them) about the man who owned the place; few were complimentary and more than one story concerned people that disappeared or suddenly turned up dead but nothing was ever proven. It is probably just coincidence, but the old man died of a heart attack just after two skeletons – each with a 45 caliber hole in the skull – were discovered in a shallow grave on the Texas side. Anyway, when Dad bought the first nineteen hundred acres on Red River, he dealt with over a dozen land owners but he turned down the beer joint and the five acres it sat on as being priced too high. Before six months passed, he went back and paid the price; there was no way that he could operate a ranch with that enterprise – and its' customers – in his midst.

The whole family came to help clean up when Dad got the beer joint bought; wc kids wcrc put to picking up beer cans and tossing them in a hole Dad had a bulldozer dig. We filled that hole up with beer cans and the dozer squashed them down three times before we ran out of cans. Dads' idea was that we would camp at the beer joint while we got it cleaned up; the only amenities consisted of an off the chart malodorous out house and a shallow well with a pitcher pump out back. Mother took one look at the set up and vetoed that plan; we stayed forty miles away at the closest motel and drove back and forth. The three room building was solid enough, made of ceramic tile with a concrete floor but it was filthy beyond belief. Dad and I tore apart and carted away the rough wooden bar that ran the full width of the cabin in the front room; an indication of the historical atmosphere of the place was that each of the windows was propped open with either a pickax handle or the big end of an eye hoe handle cut to club length. The week that we spent getting the beer joint cleaned up was not exactly a joyous family event; during the whole time, we were hot, dirty and cross. Things came to a head as we were on hands and knees scrapping away with tire tools and screwdrivers at the multiple layers of linoleum covering the barroom floor; we had been hard at the task for several hours when a rat as big as a lot of housecats dropped out of the attic and into our midst. Mother drew back and threw the tire iron she was scrapping with at the rat and let out a string of curses using words that I would not have believed that my Mama knew. We finally got the place livable without having either murder or a divorce; the old out house was bulldozed under and replaced with a brand new one painted fire truck red – it rode up from Texas as the topmost item on a truckload of materials and equipment. We camped in the beer joint when we came to Oklahoma for a number of years before Dad remodeled it with paneling, indoor plumbing, running water and a fireplace. Probably just my imagination, but even after the remodeling, I thought I could still smell the remnants of the gallons of Lysol that Mother used in the great cleanup.

The Fragrant Ford
Convertible

MY FAMILY – DAD in particular – has a love affair with practical jokes; for Dad there was no better victim than a prospective son-in-law. About 1954 my oldest sister, Cissy, brought a fellow home to meet her parents. Cissy was in school at the University of Texas in Austin and had met Pat who was a student at Texas A&M College. In those days A&M was a male only school and on Friday evening the mob of Aggies leaving campus resembled the cloud of bats leaving a bat cave at dusk. It was still that way when I enrolled two years later and for the life of me, I can't imagine why I went to an all male military school; anybody who went to A&M in those days and thought that his college days were the best part of his life must have had a miserable childhood. Anyway, being good hosts, we took Pat on one of our favorite sports – shooting jackrabbits at night from the fender of a pickup. We had a fine time and tossed fifteen or so jackrabbits into the back of the pickup for dog food. When we got back to town, Dad made a big to do about, "We forgot to drop the rabbits off at the ranch house" and how Walt should get them out and put them in the trash barrel. Cissy and Pat walked into the house and Dad lagged behind long enough to hatch a little mischief with me. When they were all in the house, I got a roll of bailing wire and proceeded to tie Jackrabbits in every available hiding place on Pats' 1950 Ford convertible; I tied them in the frame channels and to the twin exhaust pipes and everywhere else one would fit and not be obvious. I found places for all fifteen rabbits.

Next morning Cissy and Pat left to take Cissy back to UT and Pat to go back to A&M. We didn't hear anything for quite a while but eventually the story came back. Pat parked his car in the dorm parking lot and hadn't had occasion to use the car for five or six days when one of his buddies asked if he could borrow the car to go on a date. Pat said sure, gave him the keys and told him where the car was parked; about an hour later, friend comes back and gives Pat his keys. He had started out to get his date and noticed a smell when he got close to the car; he thought that something had crawled under the car and died and that he would leave the smell behind. Smell didn't let up – it got worse, a lot worse – and he brought the car back and parked it. Next morning Pat goes to check on his car and realizes that he has a big problem when the pavement under the car was alive with wiggling –crawling maggots swimming in a puddle of goo. This took place in September in College Station Texas; it was hot and it was humid. Pat got some guys to help him push the car away from the worst of the maggots but nobody helped him when he got under the car and cut loose and drug out the remains of fourteen rabbits. He would hold his breath, cut loose a carcass and crawl out to vomit and go back to do it again. It took him quite a while and he never did find the one between the radiator and the grill.

WWD 2014

It must have been true love because Pat stayed around and he and Cissy got married.

Pat was staying at Mother and Dads' house for the wedding and the morning of the big event, I took a chain and a padlock and chained him to the bed – boy slept like he was dead. Anyway Pat was still chained to the bed when the Halkus brothers – friends of Pat and members of his wedding party arrived. These are two big boys and they got me to unlock the padlock so that they could carry Pat – still in boxer shorts and tee shirt – out and chain him to a telephone pole on the side of the highway. Pat is standing there with cars coming bye and people gawking when a car stops and a fellow gets out and gives Pat some religious tracts; Pat takes the literature and the fellow says, "If you will read this and change your ways, you won't get in this kind of trouble." About this time Mother arrives to turn the water hose on me and the Halkus brothers and Pats' Dad arrives with a chain cutter to get him loose in time for the wedding.

I gave it my best but they got married and stayed married.

Tomfoolery

WORKING CATTLE IN dense brush calls for special skills and special horses but some of the wildest rides came not from cow chases but from tomfoolery like trying to rope coyotes. Dad jumped a coyote one day on the gyp lease when he was riding Redman, who could run a hole in the wind but like many of those old brush ponies tended to take the bit in his teeth and stop or turn only if it suited him. They were gaining fast and had the coyote wringing his tail and looking back when Dad looked down and realized that Redman was jumping dry washes four feet deep and six feet wide on the dead run. The fun kind of went out of the chase and Dad went from thinking about roping coyotes to begging old Red to "whoa you old fool, whoa". He finally got Red stopped but he never did get to rope his coyote. I think it kind of chapped him when, years later, I did rope one; I never did tell him that mine was a little bit crippled.

Dad had a little of that bits in the teeth attitude when it came to driving vehicles. If he could go somewhere horseback, he saw no reason he couldn't go there in his car. To be in the car with him when he jumped a coyote was a memorable event because nothing mattered except catching the coyote. We were on the Oklahoma ranch one night when we heard coyotes in the sheep. I knew better but Dad decided that he would drive, my friend Royce Ginn would run a spot light and I would get on the fender of Dads 1956 Buick Century with a shotgun and we would go to war with the coyote tribe. The sheep were grazing in a 120-acre wheat field and sure enough we were no more than through the gate until Royce picked up a coyote in the spot light and Dad let the hammer down on the Buick. Shooting jack rabbits from the fender of cars and trucks was one of our favorite sports but that Buick didn't have any place to grip with your legs so I was more or less just balancing on the hood and trying to keep my feet on the bumper. Royce had opened the passenger side door and was standing up wedged between the top of the car and the door so that he could work the spot light in all directions. The coyote was running flat out in just a few steps but he was no match for that Buick. I don't know how fast we were going but we were eating that coyote up and my eyelids felt like they were trying to roll up in the wind when we hit the only ditch in the field. The front of the car bounced up hard from the impact and I flew straight up in the air for what felt like twenty feet before landing behind the car. Royce swore that the door latched with him between it and the car before he was able to get back in and maybe it did because that door never did work right after that night. Dad pulled a tight circle and when he saw me standing up, went back to chasing the coyote. We didn't get a coyote that night but this would be the first round of what would be a forty-year tussle between me and the coyotes on that ranch.

The fight didn't end until sometime in the 1990's when I brought sheep back onto the ranch with guard dogs. The guard dogs prevented all coyote problems; we still had lots of coyotes but the dogs killed any that got in the sheep. Before long, we had a resident group of coyotes that didn't kill sheep and being highly territorial, they wouldn't allow strange coyotes – that might be killers – come onto the ranch. At this point, I stopped killing coyotes and would not let anyone else kill them; they acted like a second set of guard dogs but they still had to stay away from the sheep or the guard dogs would kill them.

The Great Coyote War

THE COYOTE HAS always fascinated mankind; every society that shares space with coyote has stories and myths describing his intelligence, adaptability and cunning. The Navajo say, "Coyote is always there and he is always hungry". The Mexican folk tales bestow the honorific "Don" to coyotes' name as a sign of respect. Ranchers by and large hate them because of their fondness of lamb, kid, and veal. Ranchers trap them, poison them, shoot them and curse them and all of their kin but every rancher at war with the coyote tribe has at least one tale that demonstrates how smart they are; these tales usually start, "You would not believe" and wind up with, "I swear that is the gospel truth."

WWD 2013

They say that when the world ends because we blew it up or poisoned it or whatever, that the only creature left alive will be the cockroach; I'm betting that coyote will be there to make supper out of cockroach.

In the winter of 1961 I moved to Oklahoma to run the family ranch on Red River. We had 1500 Angora wethers on the place that Dad had sent up from Texas and we were having hell with the coyotes. For several years we had very little coyote trouble; Dad would buy billy kids in Texas and run them out there until they were two years old before castrating them. This made a big stout wether goat that weighed about 165 pounds and was more than a single coyote wanted to tackle. We had gotten along so well that in the fall of 1959, he bought several hundred

Billy kids and sent them straight to Red River. This was a big mistake; the coyotes learned that they could kill the kids and then learned to kill the big wethers. When I got there, we were losing one or more goats nearly every night and I swung into full coyote control mode.

I had gotten some tips from a really good government trapper in west Texas and brought six wolf traps, a bunch of snares and four cyanide guns with me. I killed several coyotes before ever setting a trap just by keeping a rifle with me all the time; if I was a hundred yards or so away, coyotes would just stop and look at me since no one ever bothered them. I had the advantage that all of the perimeter fence and most of the interior fences were net wire so that coyotes crossed these fences mostly at spots where they had dug under the fences. The government trapper had impressed on me how good a coyotes' nose was so I went whole hog to keep my scent away from my sets. The pieces of canvas that I put over the trap jaws so I could camouflage them, I buried in the edge of the cow lot for a couple of days and I boiled my traps in tank water to kill any human scent. I never handled any of my trapping tools without clean cotton gloves and was very careful making my sets. I had a piece of old canvas that I put down to kneel on while I set a trap and I used it carry away the extra dirt from the trap hole. I sprinkled the area with water from a dirt tank and was not satisfied if I could tell where the trap was when I finished. I made a set one day while explaining what I was doing and why to the man who worked with me. I finished the set and was carrying my stuff back to the truck when I heard a strange sound; I turned around to find my helper peeing on a fence post three feet from the set. Homer could hit a running coyote at two hundred yards but he never did make a trapper.

Before I set the first trap, I made a tour of the fences and picked six spots where coyotes had crossed recently. I set a trap at each of the six crossings and the first night I caught four coyotes. I decided that I was one hell of a coyote trapper but truth was my success was due more to the abundance of coyotes than to my skill. At one spot where a fence crossed a drainage ditch, I caught a coyote every night for three nights straight. I caught eight or nine gyp coyotes that had all been in a trap before I caught a dog coyote; that kind of made me wonder if the government trapper that had been working the area before me was practicing a little job security. The coyotes got smarter but I learned too; that first winter I killed a lot of coyotes but the goat killing went on. I started penning the goats at night in my house yard and leaving the lights on all night. That worked for a while before coyotes came into the yard to kill a goat right outside my bedroom window and I ran over another goat with my pickup trying to get a shot at the coyotes. When we sheared goats that spring, we gave up and shipped the goats back to Texas.

Coyotes get blamed for a lot of calf deaths; I know that this happens but it is much rarer than people believe. Calves die and coyote will certainly eat any calf found dead but in all the years I was on the Red River ranch, I only knew of one calf killed by coyotes. It was bitter cold and snow had been on the ground for a couple of weeks when I found where a crippled gyp coyote and two pups fought and killed a calf. The scene was easy to read in fresh snow; the coyotes fought the calf over an area half the size of a football field before finally getting it down. I killed the gyp several days later and she was very thin and barely able to travel due to a bullet wound in a front leg.

We still had red wolves in southeast Oklahoma when I moved there and these animals could and did kill calves on occasion. They tell the story of a government trapper that worked in the area about this time; every month he sent in his report showing how many coyotes, how many bobcats and how many wolves he had caught. The official line was that the red wolf was extinct in the U.S. so the brass told trapper to quit reporting that he was catching wolves; that they were coyotes. The trapper said that he knew the difference between a wolf and a coyote and that he was going to report what he caught. The word came back from on high that from now on, anytime he caught a wolf, he was to skin it out – feet, head and all – salt the hide, boil all of the bones until they were clean and send all of this to headquarters. Would you believe that the old man never caught another wolf?

Much harder to deal with than either coyotes or wolves were the dog coyote crosses that began to show up in the early 1960's. About 1966, we began to lose weaned calves that weighed 450 to 500 pounds; there was no doubt that the calves were being killed and not just being eaten after dying from something else. Unlike the crippled coyote, these killers knew how to take down a large animal but it still entailed a fight and a lot of blood spilled over a big area. At first, I suspected wolves (I had seen a pair of red wolves harassing calves) but it had been quite some time since I had seen or heard a wolf. Coyotes and ranch dogs could be in the middle of a first class cuss fight – barking and howling at each other – but when wolf howled, the coyotes shut up and the dogs crawled under the porch.

I set traps baited with coyote urine and I set blind sets in access routes to the weaning pasture with no results except to find where a large canine detoured around my traps. The track was too big to be a coyote and was rounder than a coyote track but neither did it look like a wolf track. Over the years, I had killed several animals that appeared to be dog- coyote crosses (one had a white ring around its neck and another had floppy ears). Once I rode up on a neighbor's big black dog breeding a coyote gyp while his brother kept a male coyote at bay. I started spending time early in the morning and late in the evening in a blind on top of a barn on the edge of the pasture but again no results. The killing stopped only when a neighbor to the west shot a big dog-coyote cross and another neighbor ran over a similar animal on the road.

Hardheaded Horse

I FOUND OUT what was going through Dads' mind as Redman jumped the ditches twenty years later when my soon to be Father-in-law, Jeff Christian, asked me to go with him to gather some cattle on his Clear Boggy River bottom ranch. By the time I got there he had already caught and saddled the horses, which he had brought with him from south Texas, and he told me to ride a tall, longheaded black horse with an old sunscald scar on his rump. To reach the cattle we had to cross an area that had been cleared by sawing the timber off even with the ground so that there were stumps flush to the ground everywhere, many of them with holes in their centers just the right sizes to swallow a horses' leg clear up to his belly. Everything was fine until we struck a lope to get to the backside of the pasture; my horse didn't like being second in line so he grabbed the bits in his teeth and left the trail to pass Jeff's big grulla in a dead run. I hauled back on the reins only to find that there was no curb strap on the bits to apply pressure to the horse so he just stuck his head straight out and ran a little faster. I couldn't stop him so I pulled his head to the left to turn him, I pulled it around until that old fool was looking back at me and he was still going through the stump field at a dead run. I could see the holes in the stumps flash bye as we passed over them and decided we had a better chance if the horse could see them as well; I gave him back his head and sat real loose in the saddle ready to kick loose when he stuck a leg in one of those holes. After what seemed like an awful long ways, we got to the edge of the pasture and a brand new five-strand barbed wire fence. I was just about ready to bail off and let that hardheaded bastard hit the fence by himself when he slid to a stop with his nose right on that new fence. Jeff arrived pretty quick and was saying something about how it probably wasn't a real good idea to run a horse across that sawed ground when he saw my face and that I had broken off a piece of fence wire and was using it to make a curb for the bits. He mumbled that he couldn't imagine what had happened to the curb strap on that bridle but it put me to wondering just how bad he didn't want me to marry his daughter.

Redman and the Government Grass

ABOUT 1953, THE government came up with a program
called The Soil Bank where they would pay farmers
to plant grass on cultivated land. Dad had just bought a
half section in Fisher County that had about one hundred
and fifty acres of cultivated ground and being paid more
than he was apt to make growing cotton for doing nothing was irresistible. He signed up and Monk Hollowell
and I planted the cotton patch to grass and started building a fence around it. You could not graze the ground for
the life of the Soil Bank contract so we had to make sure
that neither the neighbors' nor our cattle could get into
the government grass. We planted the field to Sorghum
Alum, which was the latest miracle grass at the time. It
was supposed to grow ten feet tall and come back every
year from the roots. It grew ten feet tall all right but had
about as much feed value as cardboard and died out after
just a year or two; this was probably a good thing since

it also had a bad problem in that it formed Prussic acid, which poisons cattle. Anyway, when we finished building the fence the grass was about seven feet tall and thick as hair on a dogs' back. Dad had a handful of cows on the half of the place that was in pasture and I arrived one morning to find the gate open and the cows out in the government grass. We had brought Redman up from the Decker ranch so that we would have a horse if we needed one but I didn't have my saddle or even a bridle. I didn't want to drive forty miles to Decker and forty miles back so I rooted around and found an old lariat rope behind the seat of the truck and caught Redman. I made a halter with one end of the lariat, mounted Redman bareback and we sallied forth to save the government grass. Redman was getting a little long in the tooth by this time but he could still move out pretty good when it suited him. He was an old brush horse and a cow chase through thick brush was his idea of a good time. We found all the cows together on a little mud hole tank and started drifting them back along the fencerow to the gate with no problem. That is until one of those old sisters made a break into the tall grass and all of her buddies followed at a dead run bucking and snorting like a bunch of yearling heifers. I wanted to follow along slowly until they had their little romp but Redman would have none of it; those cows were running from us and he was damn well going to catch them. We plunged into the grass and it was like being under muddy water, I couldn't see ten feet in any direction but Redman could hear those cows popping the cane and was running blind right on their trail. My rope loop around his nose had no effect except to give me something to hold on to and there wasn't anything I could do but cuss Redman and go along for the ride. Even this was no problem since I knew the cows would soon tire of their foolishness and we could proceed at a more reasonable pace. We were parting that tall grass like Moses through the Red Sea when a terrible thought hit me; there was a brand new five-strand barbed wire fence around three sides of that patch that we built after the grass was planted so the grass grew right up to the fence. If we hit that fence even at an angle, at the pace we were going it would a hell of a wreck. After another bout of hauling on the rope, I finally reached up and grabbed one of Reds' ears and twisted it. This was a poor way to treat a fellow that was just doing his job and it surprised him so much that he tangled his front feet in grass and stumbled, almost going down. Before he could get his stride back, I jumped off and stopped him by wrapping my end of the lariat around my butt and hauling back. He was not pleased with me but I sweet-talked him a minute before remounting and since he could no longer hear the cattle running, we continued our cow hunt at a walk. We rode through that patch side-to-side at least three times finding trails going in all directions but no cows. No cows, that is, until we got to the fence between the government grass and the pasture, all of the old biddies were lying in the shade of a tree in their pasture calmly chewing their cuds and looking innocent as newborn babes.

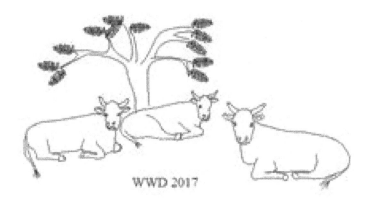

WWD 2017

Super Fertile Sheep and Other Trials of the New Ranchers

S HORTLY AFTER MOTHER and Dad married, they moved to the Decker ranch and started ranching on their own. Dad leased the Decker from his Mother and bought an adjoining half section. Like everyone else in the area he was running Hereford mother cows. At this time I doubt that there was a single bull of any beef breed except Hereford in Nolan County; a few Jersey and Holstein bulls belonging to the dairy farmers but on the range the Hereford was King. You could go to the local cattle auctions in the fall of the year and if you didn't know better, swear that they were running the same set of four hundred pound Hereford calves through the ring time after time. Mother and Dad had some grade Hereford cows but wanted to be in the registered cattle business and so bought twelve of the best, registered Hereford heifers that they could find. The heifers came bred to a really high-powered Hereford bull and Mother and Dad were

awfully proud of those little ladies. The folks had borrowed the money to buy the cattle and were determined
to take the best possible care of them. They had a pasture of their own and Dad made sure that they got plenty
to eat. Regularly he and Mother would ride out to their
pasture late in the evening and bring the girls a treat
of three or four pounds of cottonseed each or maybe a
gallon each of oats. The heifers thrived with this atten-
tion, not only growing but also getting fat. As any cowman will tell you, the prettiest color of cattle is fat and
Dad said that when they started springing with that first
calf, he had never seen a prettier set of heifers. Dreams
of pastures full of fat registered cattle turned to night-
mares though when the heifers started calving. Dad was
watching them like a hawk and saw the first one start into
labor. He watched until he knew she was in trouble and
then went to help her. It was no use, the calf was simply
too big for that fat little heifer to pass through the birth
canal and both the calf and the heifer died. This was
before country veterinarians knew how to do caesarian
sections and before it was all over Mother and Dad lost all
of the calves and all but two or three of the heifers. Dad
was devastated, aside from the loan to repay; he felt that
he had failed as a rancher. He was convinced that he had
overfed the heifers and caused all of the problems. Years

later when I was breeding heifers in Oklahoma, he never failed to caution me about getting them too fat. I have calved out a lot of heifers over the years that ranged from good living shape to town dog fat and I don't think that Dad was as much at fault as he thought. Overly fat heifers may have a little more calving trouble than normal but the vast majority of calving problems – in heifers big enough to breed – come from genetics; bulls that throw heavy birth weight calves or heifers that are abnormally shaped.

About the time Dad was struggling with the fat heifers, he was also worrying with short lamb crops. The lambs got born ok and he seldom found a dead lamb but several years in a row, by the time they were big enough to sell Dads' lamb crop was down by twenty or thirty lambs. He was pretty sure that they were not being killed and eaten completely up by predators. At this time there were virtually no large predators in the sheep and goat producing areas of Texas, no coyotes, no bobcats, no lions and very few fox or raccoons. The government had predator control people that not only trapped but poisoned predators on a large scale. Individual ranchers also worked on the predators; when

I was in high school, local ranchers funded what they called a "cat club" and paid a $250 bounty for any bobcat or lion killed in Nolan County. This was at a time when $250 was two months wages for a lot of people. If a bobcat or coyote came across Nolan County, there would be six sheepherders after him and he would never make it to the Coke County line. Eagles killed a lot of baby lambs and kids for people that lambed in the wintertime but Dad was not losing baby lambs; they were disappearing after they got up nearly big enough to wean. Dad was sure they were being stolen but he couldn't figure how or by whom. The best candidate was a neighbor that bordered the new half section but Dad could never catch him in the pasture or find any sign that he had been there. Like Herefords dominated the local cattle population, nearly all sheep in the area were Rambouillet and Dad and the neighbor both ran Rambouillet sheep. Dad had built a new net wire fence with no gates between he and the neighbor when he bought the half section and he rode that fence regularly to make sure that there was no place that sheep could leak through it. Dad had seen his sheep gather up on the fence when the neighbor was feeding his sheep nearby but the fence was sheep tight and the neighbor was too old to rope a lamb and drag it over the fence. Dad never caught the sheep thief but the stealing stopped when Mother and Dad bought out the neighbor. Dad was certain the old man was stealing his sheep but he couldn't figure out how until thirty years later.

Dad and I were riding along the fence in question after the old man was years gone when Dad suddenly stopped his horse and looked intently at the fence. He sat there a minute and then said in a conversational tone "That smart old son-of-a-bitch, that sorry smart old son-of-a-bitch". I didn't have a clue as to what he was talking about and when I asked, Dad told me the sheep-stealing story and said, "Look at that fence." I looked at the fence and didn't see anything unusual until Dad got down and stuck his hand in the hole where one of the horizontal wires had been clipped out making a six by twelve inch opening just the right size for a lamb to hop through. We looked up and down the fence and found several more of the "lamb gates" that you didn't see unless you knew what you were looking for and looked directly at it. The old sheep thief would feed his flock close to the fence and when several of Dads' lambs had crawled through the "lamb gates" to

get a bite of feed the old man would drive the flock
away and next sale day the lambs would go to market.

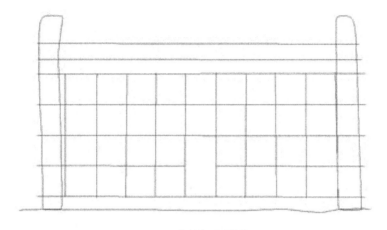

WWD 2017

More Troubles for
Young Ranchers

MOTHER AND DAD didn't have an easy time in their early married life; stolen lambs and dead cattle were bad enough but they also had other problems; like the time Dad roped a calf and stepped off his horse into a prairie dog hole. He went into the hole up to his knee and fell forward on his face; needless to say, he spent quite a while in the hospital. Mother came to bring him home but there was no way the cast would fit in the car. They solved this problem by having Dad sit in the right hand seat and stick his leg with the cast out on the running board (the doors of the car opened forward); Mother tied the door so it would not fly all the way open and they started home to the ranch. About fifteen miles from home, they ran into a downpour; it was raining so hard Mother couldn't see the road and had to stop. By the time it lightened up enough to drive, the cast was melted so back to town to get another.

Dad got mobile again and things were looking better; their Angora goats made a heavy spring clip and Dad started to town with two five hundred pound bags of mohair on his little flat bed pickup. He was doing good until he got to running a little fast coming down nine mile mountain; he made the first of several curves OK but on the second, both bags of hair rolled off the truck. There was no way Dad could reload those bags by himself so he rolled them off the pavement so someone wouldn't run into them and he went looking for help. He was lucky and found two men on the nearby Boothe Ranch to ride back and help him. They got back just in time, as they came around the curve, a Mexican shearing crew was loading his mohair. Dad didn't speak much Spanish but he was tired, hot and that mohair represented every dime he had to his name; he got his hair back.

I didn't know it until I was grown, but my sisters and I came very close to not getting born. Mother and Dad were going into town one day so Mother told Dad that if he would kill a couple of the broiler chickens that she was raising, she would dress them and they would take them in to Dads' mother. She got busy doing something else and when she looked out to see what was holding

Dad up, he had killed over fifty chickens. They had no electricity or running water so they was nothing to do but fill every tub they had with dead chickens and take them to his mothers' house where all hands spent till late night dressing chickens. I never did fine out why Dad got carried away but his stock hit dead bottom with his new wife and his mother and it was a minor miracle that the two of them hadn't run Dad off.

Things You Shouldn't Rope

IT IS A fact of life that any cowboy worth the name will
try to rope just about anything he can get close enough
to reach. A family friend, A. G. Lee told of coming down a
narrow trail on his Montana ranch and meeting a bull elk
coming up. The trail ran through a devil's club thicket and
was just barely wide enough to clear the bulls rack. A. G. was
tied hard and fast like any good brush country cowboy and
spurred up on the bull while it was getting turned around
and hooked a loop on him. The bull bailed off the mountain, the horse threw a fit and they took turns jerking each
other down for a couple of hundred yards down the mountain before the rope broke. Between them they cleared several acres of devil's club and long before it was over, all A.G.
wanted was loose.

As it was, he was luckier than the little son of his ranch
foreman who rode his Shetland pony up on a big bull moose
lying down in a swampy spot and roped him around one

horn. The moose jumped up to run and when he hit the end of the rope, jerked the pony clear off his feet. When the pony went down, the kid was thrown clear with just bumps and bruises but wound up with a bad scare and a dead pony. You could say that he was a foolish reckless little boy who didn't consider the possible results of his actions but in truth he was just a cowboy in training, training to be a foolish reckless big cowboy like the rest of us.

A time or two over the years I have bounced a loop off the rump of a deer but I never got that last few feet needed to catch one. Probably just as well, I know several men who have roped one deer but I don't know anybody that has roped two. Bud Thornberry tells of catching a buck in a sandy riverbed where his horse could out run the deer. He caught the buck but soon wondered just who had caught who? The deer would hit the end of the rope and come right back like the ball on one of those rubber band ping-pong paddles. There was no way his horse could keep facing the deer and on one trip past, the deer tangled Bud in the rope and jerked him off his horse. The horse stampeded and he and the deer went out of sight down the river still tied together. Bud found his horse a mile or so away dragging the rope but no sign of the buck.

Mr. Rocky Reagan, as fine a man as ever lived and an old time steer man, told of finding some strange tracks as he crossed a dry creek bed. This was on a ranch he was leasing in south Texas back in the 1950s. The creek bed was deep sand that didn't hold a good print so Mr. Rocky couldn't tell what had made the tracks; they looked as if something had drug a big log end ways through the sand. This got Mr. Reagan's curiosity up so he followed the trail up the creek until he came up on a really big alligator. The gator was about to make it to a pool in the creek bed so Mr. Reagan spurred up and roped it just before it made it to the water. He expected the gator to try to crawl into the water so he whirled his horse around to better pull the gator away from the pool. Problem was when the gator felt the rope; he started rolling sideways wrapping up in the rope and getting a lot closer than Mr. Rocky's horse could stand. The pony saw that rolling "whatever it was" coming and made a mad lunge to get away from it. This spun the gator in the opposite direction like a yo-yo on a string and got it far enough away that the horse checked his mad dash just in time for the gator to reverse direction, roll up in the rope and get too close again. They went through this process several times until Mr. Rocky decided that he couldn't win this tug of war and cut his rope. Mr. Gator finished rolling up the rope and waddled into the pool wearing thirty-three feet of yacht line manila lariat like sweater.

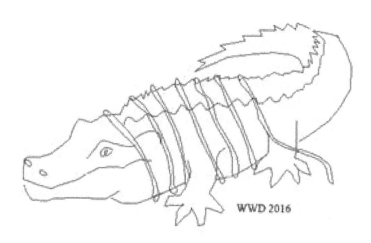

WWD 2016

It is possible that I would have been in worse shape than roping an alligator or a bull elk had I caught what I roped at going up the steep slope of Reese Canyon Mesa. I was about seventeen. I don't remember where I was going or why I had a loop built, the slope was way too steep for there to be livestock of any kind on it but I carried a built loop a lot at that age. Monkey was making headway up the slope only by lunging then gathering himself and lunging again and I was leaned forward over his neck to keep from over balancing him and we were just a few feet from the top when I looked up and saw an opportunity to go down in cowboy legend. In a shallow cave under the rim rock just ten feet above me was a turkey buzzard nest with two half grown chicks and one grown bird; the grown bird took to wing and before I had my brain in gear much less thought the situation through, I stood up in the stirrups and launched a loop at the flying bird. Had I caught the bird, there were two possible outcomes neither of which bears even thinking about. First, the buzzard could have used the standard buzzard response to danger and emptied its belly and bowels so as to fly faster or if I dodged this, I could have had a flapping, squawking, stinking monster on the end of my rope and my horse on a forty-five degree slope three hundred feet high. Evidently somebody was watching over me because I sailed the loop over the buzzards' right wing but jerked my slack before its head got in the loop so that I merely jerked the bird sideways and the loop slid off letting the bird free.

More Things You Shouldn't Rope

MONK HOLLOWELL TOLD a story of when he was work-ing for a big outfit in the Carrizozo Mountains of New Mexico. It seems that the cow boss was one of those people that nobody could please and was just down-right mean to boot. Monk and another hand topped a ridge one day just in time to see this cow boss running a pretty good sized bear across a flat below them. As they watched, he caught up to the bear, roped it and whirled his horse away from the bear intending to choke it down. Trouble was his horse was terrified of having the bear behind him and kept whirling back to face it. Monk and his buddy sat on the ridge watching and laughing as the cow boss tried everything he knew to get his horse to drag that bear. The bear had quit fighting the rope and found out that if he went toward the horse the rope loosened up; the horse didn't want the bear any closer and was backing up as fast as he could to stay away from the bear. Monk and the other rider were both carrying saddle guns but weren't about to do anything to get the cow boss out of his predicament and were hoping that he would have to cut his rope to get loose. Finally the cow boss stepped off his horse, ran to a nearby fence, broke off and ripped loose a fence post, came back and beat the bear to death with it. Monk said he still didn't like the S.O.B. but he got real careful not to push him too hard.

Monk got a little of the same medicine one time when he rode up on a badger and roped it around the head and one front leg just as it got to its' den. Monk figured he would just turn around so his horse could get a better pull and snatch Mr. Badger out of his hole. Monk said, "I was riding a hell of a good horse", I never heard him admit to riding anything else, "and was a little surprised when the rope got tight and my horse started grunting but the badger didn't come out. I touched that pony with my spurs and told him to quit fooling around and pull that badger out.

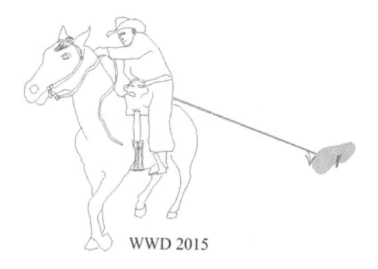

WWD 2015

He dug in and pulled till his belly was nearly on the ground and that rope started singing like a fiddle string but still no badger. Worse yet every time the horse would let up a little to get a breath, that badger would get some more of my rope. He got about six more feet, six inches at a time, before I finally saw that we were beat and got off to reach as far down that hole as I could and cut my rope. The rope end came by me so fast it like to have jerked my leggings off. If you are going to rope a badger, make damn sure you catch him where you can choke him down."

Something You Damn Sure Shouldn't Rope

DAD OWNED THE International Harvester franchise in Sweetwater, Texas and sold all sorts of hardware and ranch supplies. When I was in high school, one of my jobs around the store was to make up lariat ropes. Dad bought yacht line manila rope by the huge coil and it was my job to measure off the right lengths, tie a Turks head knot in one end, a Turks head plus a lariat loop knot in the other and stretch and coil the rope ready for sale. Nothing has the feel of a new yacht line manila lariat; a good one feels like it is alive in your hands and just demands that you rope something. It was this feel that got me into a whole bunch of trouble on my tenth birthday. I got the best birthday present ever, a brand new 33-foot 7/16ths scant yacht line manila lariat so stiff that you could hold three feet of it out horizontally. Up to now my ropes had been hand me downs that had been used till they were worn and soft with no more feel then a cotton sash rope. This new rope would coil up flat and when I shook out a loop, it stood open instead of collapsing on its self like a wet dishrag. I was standing in the back yard glorying over the way that rope felt as I swung the loop and wishing I had something besides the bucket I was roping to test my skill. There were no candidates available, no calves, no goats, nothing; even the dog had disappeared. Suddenly my little sister Judy comes running out of the house and announces that she wants to play with my new rope. The devil on my shoulder spoke up and said if she would hold her fingers up to her head like horns and run like a calf coming out of the chute, she could have a turn with the rope. She took off running and I made one, two, three swings and sailed that loop over her head and reached and jerked my slack for a perfect catch. Disaster! That new rope burned her neck and arm and when she fell, she came up squalling with a bloody nose. Mom arrived to doctor and comfort Judy but the four hours or so before Dad got home was one of the longest waits of my life. To this day Judy tells everyone who will listen that I broke her nose and the last time I saw my new rope, Dad was lifting me off the ground by swinging a three-foot double of it against my butt as he held me by one arm and I ran in a circle.

If You Rope It, You Got to Tie It

IWAS EATING supper one night in a cafe in Wichita Falls Texas when a young cowboy and his lady friend came in and sat down next to me at the counter. The boy looked like he had been in a knife fight with a circle saw, his shirt and pants were in rags and he had cuts, scrapes and bruises on every piece of hide that was visible and there has a lot of hide showing. The girl was alternating between trying to clean him up with wet napkins and giving him hell for being the stupidest man in God's creation. I didn't ask but he could see that I was about to bust to know what had happened so he grinned and told his story. They had been riding fence on a ranch south of town when a big buck deer jumped up right under their horses. He had been riding along playing with a built loop and without even thinking about it, stood up in his stirrups and sailed that loop over the bucks horns. He was slow jerking his slack though and the deer ran through the loop so that he caught him by both hind feet and jerked him down. His pony ran backwards and sat up keeping the rope tight so it seemed reasonable to grab a pigging string and go down the rope to tie that deer. The second he touched it though it was obvious that this might not be a real good idea; if he grabbed a horn, he got slashed with a front foot and if he grabbed the feet, he got slashed and jabbed with the horns. To make things worse the deer kicked his hind feet free so that now there were four feet plus the horns to contend with and the deer had quit trying to get away and had decided to open up a can of whup ass on the so and so that had disturbed his nap. They went round and round and up and down with the deer kicking, butting, slashing, everything but biting him. His wife kept screaming for him to turn the deer loose and he didn't have air enough to tell her that he had been trying for ten minutes to turn the damn thing loose. One way or another, he wound up astraddle that bucks back with a horn in each hand and the deer on top. His wife saw her chance, jumped down and tied the deer's' hind feet together with a mesquite tree between them. By the time they had caught their horses and gathered up his hat and what they could find of the stuff that had been in his pockets when they were still pockets, he decided that he didn't really want that deer. They mounted up and he reached over from the saddle to cut the deer loose and they came to town with nothing but a good tale to tell.

An Extraordinary Man

BOTH OF MY Grandfathers died before I was born and I am sorry that I didn't get to know either of them since both were remarkable men. Grandmother Trammell was a young widow who married Grandfather Trammell when he was sixty-one years old after his first wife had died several years earlier. I never got to know Grandfather, he died when Mother was only six years old but I was fortunate to be able to talk with quite a few people who knew him well. Grand Dad grew up working with his Father and brothers in Texas on what was then the frontier of civilization. There was no school available when he was a boy but later on his younger brothers and sisters did get to attend school for a while – taught by a young man named John Wesley Hardin. As a young boy, Grand Dad got a schoolteacher to scratch the alphabet on his saddle skirt so he could study it while he rode and he taught himself to read. He spent less than ninety days total in school but he died a very well educated man; even learning Greek so that he could read the classics in their original versions. He also studied engineering that he would later use to survey the best route for the Santa Fe railroad. He also used this knowledge to locate the lake named after him, which supplies Sweetwater Texas with gravity flow water. Mose Newman made the statement, "He was the only man I ever knew who was equally at ease sitting across a rosewood desk from the President of a railroad or squatting across the camp fire from a group of illiterate cowboys."

Grandfather was born on the family plantation near Van Buren Arkansas on June 22, 1848 and was brought to Navarro County Texas by his parents in 1852. Phillip, his Father, was a stockman and drover who regularly trailed both cattle and horses north into Missouri and east to New Orleans. Prior to the war, he would trail cattle, by way of the Trammell Trace (laid out by one of his ancestors), to Jefferson Texas where they would be loaded on barges and towed to New Orleans. Phillip was orphaned early in life but became a very substantial man through his livestock operations.

The family lost nearly everything as a result of the War of northern aggression and Phillip died on the trail to New Orleans in 1865 leaving Tom to finish the drive, bring his Father back to Texas and to assume the care of his Mother and eight siblings. He also continued an old family tradition by joining a "ranging company" put together for protection from Indians after the reconstructionist government gutted the Texas Rangers and left the frontier unprotected. He fought Comanche and Kiowa and was with the defenders when the Comanche made their last major raid into central Texas. There were Trammells in every war and many Indian fights from when the first American Trammell, another Thomas, got off the boat from England in 1670 right up until today. They tended to have big families and the boys were always ranging out in front of civilization and moving west as it caught up to them. They served as scouts, regular army and militia; two brothers came back from trading with the Indians on the Mississippi River to fight in the American Revolution at the Battle of The Cowpens. There were Trammells in the Shawnee, Cherokee and Creek Wars with one becoming "The Hero of Nashville" for his defense of that city. In the War of 1812, one supposedly came to the battle of New Orleans with Jean Lafitte and his "privateers" while some of his kin commanded units of rangers and militia. They fought in the Texas Revolution with at least one dying in the Alamo and some of them went to Mexico with the U.S. Army during the Mexican War. I am proud to claim kin to people like these.

Things were tough in Texas after the War; there was little money in circulation, the Comanche and Kiowa had driven the frontier back east over a hundred miles; killing, raping, stealing and taking captives to abuse and to sell. The Yankee carpetbaggers had disbanded the Rangers; disarmed the few able bodied men left and were stealing everything in reach while sanctimoniously vowing to uphold the law. Grand Dad began rebuilding the family fortunes by gathering unbranded cattle that had been running wild since their owners had gone to war or gone east to escape the marauding Indians. There were thousands of these cattle running wild that were considered to be worthless since no market for them existed. At age seventeen, Grand Dad and a cousin of about his age would take two horses apiece, a sack of coffee and a sack of salt and go down into the brush country to the south to catch wild cattle. They lived on coffee and fresh beef until they put together 250-300 head of cattle which they would then drive to Indianola on the gulf coast where they were butchered for their hides and tallow. Later Grand Dad would drive cattle back to Navarro County to build his own herds and also on to markets in the north. Mose Newman, a nephew of Grand Dad's first wife, told me this story but I had quit telling it since it was obviously impossible, with no pens and only two horses each, for two men to gather and drive out of the brush a herd of wild cattle of this size. I broke my rule to tell the story to Bud Williams, perhaps the best stockman of several generations, and his reaction was "So"? Probably Bud could do it but only if he had his wife, Eunice, to help. For the rest of us it is a case of realizing that "In those days there were giants".

The Trammell Mares

HORSES HAVE ALWAYS been important to our family; the Trammell Trace that ran from western Arkansas down into Mexico, later Texas, was laid out in the early 1800's by kin of ours driving wild horses back to the states to sell. Scandalous rumors to the contrary, I feel certain none of those horses had saddle marks or Spanish brands. My Grandfather, Tom Trammell, who was of an age to be my great grandfather as he was 62 when Mother was born, was a dyed-in-the-wool horseman. He made his money in cattle but his horses were his first love. Grand Dad raised and sold a lot of working horses for many years; his practice was to run the colts until they were full four-year olds before bringing them in to be halter-broken, ridden five saddles and sold as broke horses. Grand Dads' passion was his racehorses; his Trammell mares of west Texas were widely known and admired, as were his brothers' Trammell mares of Indian Territory. Grand Dad owned and bred mares to Dan Tucker and to Traveler both foundation sires of the quarter horse breed; family legend says Grand Dad found Traveler pulling a Fresno scraper on a railroad construction gang. Grand Dad and his brother-in-law Jim Newman's mare Pan Zareta was one of the top racehorses of her day. She won 76 of 150 races while finishing second thirty-one times and third twenty-one times. For years she held the record the fastest time at five-eighths of a mile. One of my most prized possessions is Grand Dads gold pocket watch with which he could stop clock two horses at the same time. Grand Dad prospered in Navarro County where he married Mary Jane Newman of another pioneer family. In 1880 he sold out in Navarro County and moved the family to Sweetwater Texas where he greatly enlarged his ranching operation on both owned land and on the open range. At one time he controlled most of three west Texas counties plus two ranches in New Mexico. A measure of his success was that in the great drought and blizzards of 1885-87 he lost thousands of head of cattle but it did not break him. After Mary Jane died, Grand Dad married a young widow, Mattie Mae Pierce ne Freeman, who would become our Grand Mother. In 1883 Grand Dad founded a private bank that was very successful for many years but failed in the panic of 1918. He sold nearly everything he owned to keep his depositors from losing money. He was

not legally obligated to pay this money and he died shortly after in much reduced straits but no one who knew
him would have expected him to do anything different.

WWD 2013

Roping Hogs

I HAD A friend in college who helped put his self through school roping wild hogs on the Texas Gulf coast. I remembered Boosters' hog roping tales one day when I was riding through a river bottom pasture in Oklahoma and spied a big old sow and six or eight good size shoats. They were rooting around in a little swale next to the one I was riding down. My swale was deep enough that all that was visible to the hogs was my head so they hadn't seen me and the wind was high enough that they didn't hear me. I figured that I could spur old Easy over that little rise and have a good chance at catching me a roasting pig. I built a little loop not much bigger than your hat and put an extra coil of rope with the loop to give me more weight to throw. I marked where the hogs were, hunkered down so nothing showed over the rise and very quietly walked Easy down the swale until we were directly opposite our intended victims. I goosed Easy and we jumped over the rise with me swinging my pig size loop and landed right in the middle of that mess of hogs. You never heard the like of squeals, grunts and other pig noise that exploded with hogs going in every direction including between Easy's legs. It was not until Easy sucked back through himself leaving me clutching him just behind the ears that I realized that he hadn't had a clue that there was anything over that rise much less a whole herd of something's that he had never smelled, heard or seen in his whole life. Scared gave way to mad in a hurry and Easy bawled, swallowed his head and went to bucking like he wanted to beat me to death against the saddle.

WWD 2013

I'm pretty sure that the man who named Easy did so because it was real easy to decide you would rather buck down than take the beating that it took to ride him when he got into his serious pitching. He could hit the ground about as hard as any horse I ever rode and you never knew which leg was going to hit first. I had blown a stirrup right off the bat and barely managed to get back more or less in the saddle but it didn't feel good. I was seriously considering kicking loose and letting Easy have his mad fit without me when I realized that the pig sized loop was around my neck and one arm while the other end of the rope was tied hard and fast to my saddle horn. They say incentive produces performance and I suddenly had a whole bunch of incentive to ride that horse until I could get that loop off. I started off cussing him but right quick changed to begging; I'd like to think I rode that old pony to a standstill through skill but, in truth, I think he finally just got hot and quit.

Easy

YOU KNOW HOW some horses you just know that you can ride? Easy was one that I knew damn well that I couldn't ride if he put his mind to bucking me down and yet for one reason or another, he never threw me. One day I rode him up to a wagon that Don Reese was loading with Bermuda grass roots just as Don pitched a big forkful of roots up from the other side. Neither Easy nor I had known Don was there and that big glob of roots flying up out of nowhere us scared us both. I jerked and flinched a little but Easy gave his standard reaction to anything that he didn't like, he downed his head and turned it on. Don heard the commotion and came around the wagon to watch Easy buck a big circle out into the pasture and finally ease up and let me ride him back up to the wagon. Don allowed it was a hell of a ride and that he hadn't had any idea I could ride like that. If I had been honest, I would have told him that Easy had thrown me a half dozen times and just kept bucking back under me. As it was

I just grinned and went about my business. I think it was one of the few times I ever put a good ride on a pitching horse and had an audience. Make a good ride and there is nobody in five miles but buck down and everybody and their dogs will be there to see it and laugh at you.

Easy wasn't a bad horse but he had strong opinions about what a cow horse should and should not have to put up with; at the top of his should not list was kids. He never offered to kick or bite one of our little girls but he made it plain that baby-sitting was not in his job de-scription. There was no way that he would stand to have kids put up on his back even when he was tied up or for the short walk back to the saddle shed and unsaddling. One day when Colleen, our oldest, was about seven she wanted to go with me to the pasture, she asked me to ride somebody else besides Easy but I told her not to be silly and reached down to pull her up behind me. Easy goated a couple of times when we started off but I slapped him on the neck and told him to straighten up, he blew rollers in his nose and slung his head but stepped on out. When we got where we were going I got off to open the pasture gate; I was still limber enough at that time to throw a leg over the horses' neck and step off leaving Colly behind the saddle. Easy kind of danced around looking back when he realized that Colly was on his back by herself but I pulled him through the gate and told him to cut it out. When I got back on I could tell that he had a mad building so I kicked him up to a lope to let him work it off. Everything was fine until we jumped a little ditch and my fountain pen flew out of my shirt pocket, I pulled up and got off to get my pen. As I turned my back, I heard Easy bawl and whirled back hauling on the reins but it was too late. Colly when up like a sky rocket and I jumped to catch her before she came down but either she didn't go as high as I thought or else I moved too slowly because she landed on her bottom with a thump. I wanted to scoop her up and hold her but was terrified to pick her up; so I was just kneeling there beside her when she gulped a couple of times like she had the wind knocked out of her, smiled and said "I'm OK Daddy". When I quit shaking and stopped hugging my daughter, I looked around for my horse. He was standing not ten feet from us, ground tied and looking like the proverbial scatological infatuated canine; I swear that horse knew that he had just torn his britches big time. I went over to him and in a very low voice explained just how close he was to becoming the featured attraction at a coyote poisoning. He didn't move a muscle as I swung up or even when I coaxed Colly to let me pull her up behind me. We went home without incident but Colly insisted on getting down every time that I did and I didn't object but I believe at that point Easy would have carried a whole kindergarten class without objection.

Dividend

A NOTHER HORSE THAT we had about the same time was the exact opposite when it came to kids. My Father in law, Jeff Christian, gave Dividend to us after the horse had been given to him. Dividend was a thoroughbred that could run but didn't like the crowds and would come unglued any time he got in a crowded situation. My Wife, Diann, found this out when she took Dividend for her and our youngest, Kelly, to ride in a homecoming parade. I didn't go with them because by this time I had sworn off parades and they got home without anyone getting hurt only because Diann was a first-rate rider. The horse went wild when they got into the crowd and it was all Diann could do to control him until she could get him back in the trailer. He also didn't care much for cow work, Diann was riding him one day helping me gather a pasture when he threw a fit and tried to throw her. Like her Daddy, Diann could always find a reason that it wasn't the horse's fault and refused to let me get on him to teach him some manners. He would pitch with me anytime I tried to make him work and it just wasn't worth the hassle to mess with him.

Where he did shine though was with the kids. I came home one day to find Dividend standing in the front yard with all three of our little girls on him bareback, two bread sacks full of sandwiches and cookies, a thermos bottle and a plastic bottle of Kool-Aid on cords draped over his withers, three dogs barking and running circles around the horse and D.C., the pet coon, doing her best to climb up his leg to go on the picnic. As I watched, Quinn got down to hand the coon up to Colly then she climbed Dividends' front leg and the expedition got under way.

Ringo

MOST HORSES SEEM to know that kids are special. I bought a horse once that had been spoiled and was bad to kick; I found out later that he damn near killed the man that spoiled him. Anyway I had only ridden him a few saddles and we were still dubious about each other when I rode up a neighbor's house and tied Ringo in the front yard while I visited. As I walked out to leave, my heart jumped clear up into my throat when I saw their little two year old girl toddle up to Ringo and hug him around a hind leg before anyone could move. Ringo looked back to see what was happening but stood still as a statue as I gathered up the little girl and handed her back to her mother. Ringo wasn't really big enough and was always hard headed and ugly as homemade soap but he made points that day and turned into a pretty good horse. He loved to run coyotes and I was riding him the day I finally managed to rope my coyote. I caught and killed the coyote and on the way back to the pens we saw an otter in the shallow water of Tishy Lake. The waterweeds were thick enough that the otter couldn't swim under water and was jumping up over the weeds in an effort to get to deep water and away for us. I rode Ringo out into the lake and tried to time the jumps of the otter. He came up in a shallow arc and I pitched a loop over him but couldn't jerk my slack fast enough to do more than just pull his tail; still and all not a bad day for tomfoolery.

Ringo was bare footed when I bought him and badly needed to have his feet trimmed. I got him home and found out why he was long footed, he absolutely refused to let me pick up a foot and would throw a wall eyed kicking fit any time I tried to trim him. The man I bought him from did tell me to watch him, as he would kick. He was also hard to get on; I had to cheek him to mount. I was wondering if I hadn't made a mistake buying him but I was short of horses and kept working with him. He was hard headed but he wasn't dumb, he decided that he would rather let me pick up his feet then to have me trim them with him lying on his back with all four feet tied together and he learned quickly that kicking at me was not acceptable behavior.

I was doing a lot of quiet sorting taking out young pairs from the calving trap and riding piggy heifers in and to my surprise Ringo took to this work as if he liked it and quickly became a solid using horse. He was the perfect example of what happens when the man breaking a horse doesn't have as much sense as the horse.

Roany and the Locust Patch

ONE SUMMER WHEN I came home from college, Monk Hollowell, who was working for Dad part time on the Decker ranch, told me that there were two long yearling heifers in the leased pasture we called the Joe T that he had not been able to get back with the herd. There was a small creek bottom field on the Joe T but most of the pasture was thick brush and rough with Oak Creek winding through it. My little sister Judy said she would help me and we set out to capture the two outlaws; I was riding Monkey and she was on her big tall barrel racing horse Roany. Today after fifty years of experience and having being exposed to Bud Williams and some other great stockmen, I believe that I could go into that pasture, find the heifers and by working slowly and thoughtfully drift them back to the other cattle. At twenty years old though, I was a sure enough "brush cowboy" and ready to bring those heifers out at a high lope. The gate out of the Joe T into the Reese Canyon pasture of the Decker ranch was in the southeast corner of the Joe T and there was a clearing of maybe five acres right around the gate. Several times Monk had gotten the heifers into the clearing but each time they would break back either north or west into the brush before he could get them through the gate. I told Judy that most likely that I would bring the heifers up one fence or the other and that I would holler before we got to the clearing so she would know from which direction we were coming and could be ready to block the other escape route. I left Judy and Roany in the clearing around the gate and went looking for the two heifers. I found them grazing in the little field and was surprised when they spooked like a couple of deer and hit the brush the moment they saw me. Monkey and I hit the brush right behind them and the chase was on. The heifers headed for the thickest brush in the pasture with Monkey and I right on their butts; we pushed them hard on the theory that we could maintain the fast pace longer than the cattle and they would get tired and quit. We made a complete circle of the pasture and the heifers were hot and beginning to slow down when they fell off down a brush choked gully into the creek bottoms. The gully had a deep channel just wide enough for a horse to get through and was steep enough that once you were in it, there was nothing to do but go to the bottom; halfway down, a mesquite limb as big around as my lower leg appeared blocking the path just over saddle horn high. Monkey was falling as much as he was running and there was no time for me to do anything except get my hands up to try to ease some of the shock and we hit the tree going wide open. To this day, I don't know exactly what happened but when the wreck was over; Monkey was on his knees facing up the draw from where we came and I was still in the saddle holding eight feet of mesquite log crosswise in my lap. Monkey got back to his feet and shook but then had to back out of the gully; it was too tight for him to turn around. When we got on level ground, I got down checking for damage and as far as I could tell, nothing important was broken on either of us. I had a sore belly that would have a spectacular bruise the next day but aside from that, we both were fine.

By this time the heifers were long gone so I rode out on the creek bank and listened to see if I could hear them; either they had quit running or had put enough distance between us to mute the noise because there were no sounds of running cattle. As I started to ride on, I heard a very faint call, "Walt-Walt" coming from the north. I rode toward the sound and hollered every few minutes to stay on track and eventually saw Judy's horse Roany, head down in a honey locust patch; he was doing his best to follow Judy who at this point was crawling through the thorns on her hands and knees. Honey locusts grow in west Texas only in creek bottoms and other places that get extra water but they have some of the sharpest and biggest thorns around; to make it worse, the thorns are poisonous which makes the pain of any puncture more intense. The trees have an open growth habit so that sunlight can reach into the thickets and they usually have a crop of green briars growing with and on them. This makes the thickets about as easy to get through as a barbed wire jungle. I tied my horse and extricated Judy from a jumble of locust and green briar thorns and then went back to get Roany. I had to use my pocket knife to cut the ropes of green briars that had him completely trapped. We all three lost some blood and some hide and for that day, we lost the heifers. Judy came to help me and learned an important lesson for brush cowboys; you ride around the locust thickets.

Work Stock

O NE OF MY earliest recollections is reaching through a plank fence to pet something and seeing a big set of teeth coming at me; years later Dad told me what prompted this memory. He had what was known as a "government jack", an American Mammoth Jackass that the government bought and leased out to farmers and ranchers so that they could breed better mules from their work mares. Since he was both black and a jack, Mother had named the animal "Pershing" as in Blackjack Pershing. Pershing was an evil tempered old devil that Dad had to watch like a hawk to keep from being hurt or killed. I have a picture of Dad holding Pershing on a lead rope and Dad didn't take his eye off of Pershing even to get his picture taken. Anyway when I was about three, I followed Dad down to the pens and reached through the fence to pet Pershing. Dad saw me out of the corner of his eye and managed to snatch me back just before Pershing bit my arm off; shortly thereafter he sent Pershing back to the government.

WWD 2015

Dad told a story on himself about another stud. When he and Mother were first married, they had a team of work mares named Maude and Molly. Dad decided to raise colts out of these mares so when Molly came in season, he took her to the studhorse. The stud was a tremendous Perchon that began to squeal, kick the sides of his stall and generally raise hell as soon as he smelled the mare. The stud horse owner told Dad to put the mare into a big pen with high board fences and he would turn the stud in with her. Dad allowed that Molly had never been with a stud and that he would hold her to keep her from being so nervous. The man said he didn't think that was a good idea but Dad led Molly out into the pen and was petting her and rubbing her face to calm her down. The studhorse man said "Son you had better get out of that pen" and Dad said "No, I am going to hold her." At that the man said "OK" and turned the studhorse out. The studhorse came charging out into the big pen with fire in his eyes and squealing like a banshee and suddenly went up on his hind legs. He was walking toward Dad and Molly on his hind legs taking six feet at a step, squealing and pawing the air ten feet up with front hooves the size of bushel baskets and blowing slobber down on them like a rain. I asked what happened next and Dad said, "Molly and I decided that that she could take care of herself and didn't really need me."

Dads' Uncle Oscar farmed with mules and told a story that would sound like a tall tale had he not had the missing digit to give evidence. Uncle Oscar had one big mule that seemed to live solely to make Oscar's life miserable. He was the best mule Oscar owned once he was in harness and hooked up but getting him there was always a fight. He was hard to catch even in the pen and Oscar usually had to rope him to catch him. After he was caught, he was hard to bridle and would stick his nose straight up so Oscar couldn't get the bits in his mouth until he twisted an ear to get his head back down. Even bridled and wearing harness he wouldn't give up and would usually find some way to get tangled in the tugs or to get one leg over the doubletree or something before finally going to work. One morning he had been particularly ornery and both he and Oscar were mad by the time Oscar started to bridle him. He got the bridle on after an even worse than usual fight and when he reached to fasten the throatlatch, the mule whirled his head and bit Oscar's left thumb off right at the hand. He was so mad that he drew back intending to hit the mule in the side of the head but the mule swung his head so that Oscar hit the bits and broke his right hand all to pieces. With a thumb gone on one hand and the other hand broke, Oscar allowed that no man ever won a fight with a mule.

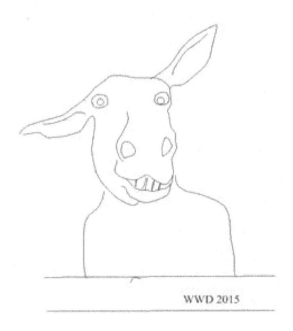

WWD 2015

Rabies

I HAD GONE to the Tishy Lake pasture one day to pen a set of cows and was riding down the edge of the timber when a coyote stepped out of the timber up ahead of us. Ringo, the horse I was riding, hadn't seen the coyote nor had my cow-dog Macho so I built a loop and kicked Ringo into a run to cut the coyote off from the timber. The dog and the horse both spied the coyote and took to him hard as they could go. The coyote was walking away from us acting kind of funny and we were within 100 yards or so before he turned and saw us coming. Macho was in the lead with Ringo and me close behind when he turned and instead of breaking to run, he started barking and growling and came to us at a dead run but kind of staggering as he ran. Things happened in a hurry when that coyote started raising hell, the little bunch of cattle that we had come to get stampeded back toward the pens bawling like the devil was after them, Macho slid to a stop then swapped ends and took off after the cattle and

Ringo whirled to follow so fast that I almost lost my seat. Dog, horse, cattle and me, I was the last one to realize that we had found a rabid coyote. The coyote followed us but more slowly, stopping ever once in a while to howl then coming on barking and growling as he came. From the time I was a little kid, Dad had a rule that you never for any reason ran a horse back to the pens; I broke that rule pretty bad that day getting back to the pens and the rifle in my truck. I like to think that I didn't really make the horse run back to the pens; I just sort of let him.

It was almost a mile to the pens and the coyote just kept coming and was still in sight when I turned into the lane leading into the pens. When I got there the cattle were crowded into a wad in the back corner of the front pen and I could hear the coyote still coming but a ways back. I turned Ringo loose in the pen, shut the gate and headed for the pickup and my rifle. When I opened the truck door, Macho dove in but down on the floorboard instead of taking his normal place on the passenger seat. I admit that I felt a mite braver when that truck door closed and I jacked a shell into the chamber of my rifle. We went back looking for the coyote but never saw nor heard it again.

Some More Rabies

I HAVE SEEN and killed a lot of rabid animals over the years but that was only the second time that I was chased by one. The first time was in the summer of 1959 when Dad and I drove up to the headquarters of the Decker ranch to find Monk Hollowell shouting at us from inside the ranch house. A mad dog had chased him into the house and came after him again every time he tried to get to his pickup. We looked around everywhere that we could see from the truck and then got out to look in the pens and barns. We both had our pistols and had about decided that the dog had either left or died when we stepped around the barn to see a big yellow dog about 75 feet away coming to us in a hurry. I don't remember this one making any noise but it was obvious that he wasn't coming to have his ears scratched. Dad and I were about twenty feet apart on a line at right angles to the mad dog. I don't know who shot first but we were both shooting and it was like the dog was running in slow motion; I could see bullets hitting him but he kept on coming. Just as I thought I was going to have to club him with an empty pistol, he turned and I fired my last round at him broadside. Dad still had shells and I heard him shoot several more times while I was trying to reload and finally heard the dog yelp as a bullet hit him. I got reloaded and shot four or five times as the dog ran away from us but it would have been a miracle had I hit it at that distance. We got over our shaking spells, gathered up Monk and went looking for the dog with no luck. Monk saw buzzards the next day and found him dead in the brush about 200 yards from where we last saw him.

Dad and I got into rabies trouble again on the Oklahoma ranch. We were gathering cows from the timber when I heard Dad holler for me to come to him. I found him at the edge of Tishy Lake with a cow out in the water on the end of his rope. He had thrown her into the bunch several times but she kept coming back to the lake until he got mad and roped her. She was sulled in the shallow water and he told me to rope her and help him pull her out. His rope wasn't tight but the cow had a funny look about her and all of a sudden started choking and went down in the water. Her head went under so I threw by billfold up on the bank and waded out to hold her head out of the water. I managed to get her head above water but she was struggling and choking and after several hard spasms, died. We drug her out of the water and I suddenly remembered what was funny about the cow; aside from choking like she had something hung in her throat, her tail was hanging limp just like a soft rope blowing in the wind. Too late, I remembered one of my professors, Dr. Redmond, telling the class that a tail totally lacking in muscle tone was a good sign of rabies in cattle. We had both gotten her saliva all over us and I had even stuck my hand down her throat to see if something was stuck there cutting off her wind. I cut her head off and took it to town to be sent off to check for rabies. Sure enough in a few days our vet called me and said he had prescriptions for both of us to start a series of rabies shots, the cow died of rabies. At that time, the series was something like twenty-one shots so they gave them under the skin on the belly where there was plenty of room. They made the area around the shot sore as hell. It wasn't too bad until about the seventh or eighth shot when a new nurse jabbed the needle straight in and squirted the vaccine onto my guts. I tried to grab her hand when I realized what she has doing but she fought me off long enough to finish the shot. She got huffy when I told her that the shot was supposed to be subcutaneous. I went to my in-laws home where we were spending the weekend and in an hour was in shock. They covered me with blankets until I quit shivering and I was all right in five or six hours but you can bet that I made sure the rest of the shots went under the skin.

Red Headed Trouble

OUR DAUGHTER QUINN is like her Grandfather Jeff in that she doesn't believe that any horse would intentionally hurt her and over the years this caused me more than a few gray hairs. The first time was when Quinn was about five and the whole family was going down to the lower pens to see La Mosca's new baby colt. I went into great detail how everyone would have to be quiet and not get too close to the new baby or startle the mare. When we went into the corral, La Mosca was across the pen facing away from us nursing her colt. Before I could move, Quinn dashed past me and ran right up to the mare. La Mosca saw something charging her baby and kicked with both hind legs like a mule; Quinn came flying back ten feet through the air. She hit the ground rolling and jumped up unhurt before I could even get to her; she had been so close when the mare kicked that she was shoved instead of being kicked and didn't even have a bruise. It would be nice if I could say that from then on Quinn listened to her Daddy but that would be too big a lie even for this set of tales.

It wasn't long after the La Mosca affair when we all went down to Red River to go swimming; on the way I told everybody that no one was to go in the water until I had a chance to wade out and make sure it was safe. We got out of the truck at the riverbank and before I could get my boots off, Quinn dashed past me and jumped in the river. She went completely under and come back up screaming "Daddy", my heart stopped when I saw that she had a fishhook from a trotline hanging from her right eye. I hollered, "Don't move" and to her credit she stood as still as a statue as I got to her and took the pressure off of the line on the hook. I was about to cut the line on the hook and dash to the doctor when I saw that the point of the hook was between the eyelid and the eye and hadn't penetrated either one. I very carefully took the hook out while holding her eye open and could not find even a scratch.

I am pretty sure that Quinn's guardian angel must have qualified for combat pay and early retirement because this happened before she was six years old and this was only the beginning. Like the time she got a pair of toy spurs for Christmas – for sure not from her Mother or me – and was all fired up to try them out on Dividend. I vetoed that idea right quick and forbid her to wear them when she went riding. About a week later Homer Gilbert, who worked with me on the ranch, told me that Quinn rode Dividend up to him to show him her new spurs, Homer told her she had best be careful, that if she made him mad with those spurs, Dividend would throw her. Quinn laughed and rode off, when she got about 100 yards off she set those spurs in Dividend and he threw her higher than an Alabama moon. Homer got to her quick as he could but she already had the spurs off when he got there and begged him not to tell her Daddy.

Or there was the time when the insurance adjuster came to inspect the hail damage on our house roof and was a little surprised to find skateboard tracks running from the roof peak down to the eve. Quinn, who had crawled up on the roof with him confessed that she was the culprit; she would ride the skateboard down from the peak and jump off onto the roof just before the board went off the roof. Or the time, when she was about fifteen, she rode her mare across the concrete dam on Blue River – where she had been forbidden to go – and the mare slipped on the concrete and slid into the water upside down. Quinn jumped off but the mare was hung up on some big rock with her head under water and couldn't roll over. The horse was frantic kicking and struggling but unable to get her head up. Quinn jumped in and held the mares' head above water for ten or fifteen minutes until some men working nearby heard her screaming and managed to roll the mare over into deep water where she could swim out. Quinn was scraped and bruised with strained muscles in her back and so sore she couldn't move but the mare was ok.

It wasn't always just Quinn being Quinn. Things happen to Quinn; like the time when she was about four, riding Tony the pony, and went to the pasture with me. I was just doodling around putting some saddle time on a green broke mare and when we passed a big tank, Tony decided to go swimming. He went right out into the deep water until nothing but his nose was above water and Quinn was screaming "Daddy". I told her to kick loose and float but to hold on to the saddle horn until I could get to her. The bronc I was riding wouldn't take the water so I finally kicked off my boots, threw my billfold down and swam out to get Quinn, just another little story to add to the Iliad of Quinn.

Monkey and the Big Parade

DIANN'S WRECK WITH Dividend at the parade reminded me of the one and only parade that I ever rode in. I was about sixteen and decided that I should load my horse Monkey in the pickup and go to the big stock show and rodeo parade in Abilene Texas. Monkey didn't like to ride in the pickup and had a tendency to climb out over the stock racks when the mood struck him. I solved this problem by bolting a D ring low on each side of the outside of the pickup bed where I could tie a rope, take a half hitch on the saddle horn and tie off to the D ring on the other side. This with a heavy rope halter tied to a ring in the front of the bed usually kept Monkey in the truck if I could get him loaded. To be fair Monkey's only problem was that as a three year old he got turned over to a kid who considered himself to be one hell of a cowboy when in reality, I knew just enough about training horses to be dangerous. We both survived and in spite of me Monkey became a good all around using horse and pretty fair calf roping horse. But to get back to the story, we arrived where the parade was forming up; I found a ditch to back into so Monkey wouldn't have to jump down and we unloaded and mounted up ready for the parade. Monkey was nervous but there were lots of strange horses to check out, the gravel road was not that different from the footing he was accustomed to and it looked as if the country horse might be okay on his first trip to town. All that ended when the band in front of us struck up with a full load of brass and drums; Monkey whirled and plunged back the way we had come shouldering horses aside right and left and not endearing us to their riders. I got him under control and could follow along with the parade so long as we stayed well back from the band but he was jumpy as a long tail cat in a room full of rocking chairs and shying at every new sight and sound. We got to the paved street and when Monkey stepped on that slick pavement and slipped almost down, he decided enough was enough and went to pitching. I don't know if he was mad or scared or both but he turned it on; if I pulled his head up he would lose his footing and go down and if I gave him his head he would go back to bucking. We bucked through the riders ahead of us and then into the back of the band, I squalled for them to get out of the way and we scattered band members in all directions

– including up on to the sidewalk – then we went up on
the sidewalk and chased them back into the street. We
cleared the band and there up ahead were several convertible cars with rodeo queen candidates in pretty dress-
es riding along on the top of the back seats waving at the
crowd. The last car in line was a little sport car that was
real low to the ground and it looked as if Monkey was
going to buck right into the car in spite of all I could do.
The boy driving looked back to see us barreling down
right on top of them and stepped out of the car and ran
leaving the girl and the little car rolling down the street.
I managed to pull Monkey around the car at the last minute and turned him down a side street away from the
parade. I have wondered a lot of times over the years how
that boy explained his behavior to his girlfriend.

When we got away from the crowd Monkey settled
down some but he was still nervous and tip toeing along
on that slick pavement like a hog on ice. We made it back
to the pickup and for once Monkey was happy to load
right up. I got his halter on and the tie ropes fixed and
we were ready to go home when a string of firecrackers
went off and Monkey threw a fit trying to climb out of the
pickup, he got one foot on top of the cab and beat it in a
little and whopped Don Brian on top of the head when

he jumped out of the pickup but was about ready to settle down when a "good Samaritan" decided he was choking and before I could stop him cut the halter and tie ropes. Monkey climbed right over the racks, down over the cab and away down the street he went. I grabbed a catch rope and went after him afoot but I would have never caught him if he hadn't run into a fenced back yard. He wouldn't let me come up to him but I got close enough to rope him and then he came to me. Trouble was he came to me to reach out and bite me on the side of the belly and shake me like a dog killing a rat. His teeth finally snapped off the roll of hide he had between his teeth; though at the time I thought that he had bitten a plug clear out of me. I got a war bridle on him with the lariat and we got out of the rose garden where I caught him before the lady got to us with her broom. We finally made it home with nothing worse on either of us then my bit side and decided that our parade going days were over. It was a long time before I went back to Abilene.

A Man Called Horse

Dad got stuck with the name "Horse" when he was in high school because he could run like a horse, at six feet tall and a hundred and ten pounds he could run all day. He could run but was some lacking in the muscle department and this became a problem when the class bully decided to whip him every afternoon after school. Dad tried but he just couldn't handle the bully and he was getting tired of being whipped up on. One morning walking to school, he arrived at a plan. He found a good stout club in a stack of mesquite firewood and laid it on a ledge above where the sidewalk ran under the railroad viaduct. That afternoon when the bully started his "I'm going to whip your ass" routine, Dad broke character by running instead of trying to fight. The bully and his sidekicks followed screaming like a pack of wolves while Dad carefully loped along keeping just out of reach. When he reached the viaduct, Dad grabbed up his club and waited just around the corner. Sure enough, the bully was in the lead and came around the corner to catch the club right between the eyes. He went down like a pole axed steer and Dad put in two or three more licks for good measure. When the bully came around, Dad told him "I still can't whip you in a fair fight but I can by God knock your head off with a club if you every come at me again". He never did.

Quinn may have come by her personality honestly, her Grand Dad Davis had been known to get in a scrape or two his self and for a smart man he could do some awfully dumb things. We left the Decker headquarters one day going to do something and were in a slow lope side by side crossing an old field with lots of sandburs when all of a sudden Dads' horse was running loose and Dad wasn't on it. I looked back just in time to see him rolling head over heels and come to a stop holding up a jackrabbit by the ears. He had looked down to see the rabbit squatted down behind some weeds and decided to bulldog it. He was skinned up with grass burs stuck all over him and the rabbit was dead from getting rolled on. While I was picking grass burs out of him, I asked him what the hell he was thinking; he shrugged with a kind of silly grin and said "It seemed like a good idea at the time".

Not unlike bulldogging jackrabbits was the fall Dad took one time when we were gathering up the last few goats that took to the brush rather than being driven into the shearing pens with the flock. We usually had to catch a dozen or so of the big mutton goats and haul them in, as they would scatter as soon as they realized that we were penning goats. I had roped a goat and dragged him up in front of my saddle to take to the trailer when I looked up to see Don Bryan and Dad coming single file down a steep draw off the Reece Canyon wall after a goat. Don was in the lead and using good sense by taking it slow in the bad footing when Dad shouldered past him on Major, hell bent to catch the goat. As I watched, Major lost his feet, turned a complete somersault with Dad still in the saddle and they wound up in a pile at the base of the draw. I dumped the goat I was carrying and broke into a run to get to Dad but before I could get there, he and Major were up and had caught their goat. They both had lost hide but nothing seemed to be broken on either of them and Dads' only comment was to ask why I had turned my goat loose.

Dad seemed particularly prone to lapses in good sense when hunting rattlesnakes. Sweetwater Texas is home to one of the oldest and biggest of the rattlesnake roundups and Dad and his buddies always had a big time hunting for new dens and catching snakes. The technique is to scout likely spots like holes back under a cap rock until rattlers are seen sunning outside the den. When a promising den is found, mirrors are used to reflect light back into the holes and someone will get down close and run a piece of copper tubing back into the entrances to the den. A pump-up sprayer is used then to spray gasoline into the den making the snakes come out to get fresh air. As the snakes come out, they are caught with a variety of homemade snake catchers; Roy Jennings makes some of the best, and put into tow sacks or barrels to be taken live into the roundup check-in station. Here they are weighed, counted and measured for the biggest and smallest snake contests and put on display in a snake-pit. The tourists watch the snake handlers catch and milk rattlers while they eat fried rattlesnake and tell each other that "it tastes just like chicken". Later the snakes will be milked of their venom and slaughtered for the meat, rattles and hides. But back to Dad and the hunting; he was forever having close calls but never got bit. It is unbelievably hard to see snakes in the rock and grass around the dens and the danger, I guess, is part of the appeal. Roy Jennings tells of one time when Dad couldn't reach the hole that he wanted to gas so he lay down on his back and scooted back about twelve feet into a cave just high enough to clear his body. He was threading the tubing into a hole when Roy saw a big snake coming out of a crevice right next to Dad's side. Roy told Dad to freeze as the snake was already within striking distance. Dad lay perfectly still as the snake crawled over his chest and back into another part of the den and then he proceeded to gas the den.

The Grape Arbor Goats

MOTHER AND DAD moved to the Decker Ranch soon after they were married and Dad was a little worried about Mother being by herself while he was working since they had no telephone and no close neighbors. Wetbacks – currently known as undocumented guest workers – from Mexico would follow the creek and often came up to the ranch house looking for work. Most of these people were no problem; when a man walks 250 or 300 miles, he is looking for work not mischief. Usually they would hang back in the brush until they saw a man before coming out but Dad still worried. One summer day something happened that made Dad a lot less fearful. The lady who lived in the house before Mother and Dad, planted several grape vines and trained them to grow up and over on a grape arbor. The vines had to be watered by carrying water from the windmill but the arbor made one of the few spots of real shade in the yard and was Mother's pride and joy. Problem was they had inherited five or six Spanish goats when they bought the ranch and the goats had a real sweet tooth for grapes and grape leaves. After she had run them out of the grape arbor for the umpteenth time, Mother declared that the goats had to go. Dad promised that he would catch them and get rid of them but he was real busy trying to get fences fixed and with all the other stuff that just had to be done first. It rocked along like this for a while until one day Dad rode in from the pasture and was met at the corrals by the two wetbacks that he had hired to brush fences. They were both talking a mile a minute and as Dad said "Both of their eyes were so big that their faces looked like two fried eggs in a skillet". The Mexicans didn't have any English and Dads' Spanish wasn't very good but he did catch "muerte (dead) and pistola" and he took off at a dead run for the house with the two hands right behind him. About half way there Mother came out into the yard so he knew that it wasn't her that was "muerte" and shortly after that Dad began to pass dead goats. It seems that Mother finally hit the boiling point when she looked out and saw the goats once again after her grapes, she grabbed Dads' Colt pistol that he told her to keep handy and went to war with the goat tribe. Three of them didn't make it out of the grape arbor and the rest were strung out in a line going north. After it was all over, Dad decided that it was a pretty good day; he didn't have to worry about catching the goats, the wetbacks got full of goat meat and he felt a lot better about leaving Mother alone as her fame as a "pistolera" spread.

Bronc Riding Cotton Picker

WHEN MOTHER AND Dad took over the Decker Ranch there was a patch of cotton down in the creek bottom that they agreed the former owners could harvest. Most of the crop had been picked but a man came to the house one-day saying that he was supposed to finish picking but that he didn't know where the patch was located. Dad was about to go to the pasture and told the man that he would give him a ride to the patch. Dad was riding a big long legged white horse that had tried several times to throw him but he had ridden him and was feeling pretty cocky. He mounted and told the cotton picker to hand him his water jug and cotton sack and then he could climb up behind. The cotton picker was dubious but finally handed up his stuff and clambered up behind Dad. The horse was not at all happy about carrying double but started off at a trot with just a little hump in his back. Things might have been fine but the cotton picker decided he was falling off, grabbed Dad around the waist and started squalling for Dad to stop and let him off. As he tried to get down, he evidently hung a heel in the horse's flank because before he could get off, the horse blew up. Cotton picker made about two jumps before flying off backwards over the horse's rump. The horse had his head down and was turning it on pretty good but with the cotton picker loose from the death grip that he'd had on his middle Dad felt sure he could ride him. He was about to get control of the situation when he lost hold of the water jug; it sailed about fifteen feet high before exploding like a bomb on the ground right under the horse's nose. Turns out that the old pony had not showed Dad near all his tricks, he bawled and went into some serious pitching. Dad rode him several jumps before getting out of time and going up like a balloon. He said that he could remember to this day looking down and watching, like a slow motion movie, that horse pitching in a circle with the strap of the cotton sack hung on the saddle horn and all nine feet of it streaming out behind him like a circus banner. Dad found the cotton picker another gallon jug for water; the man thanked Dad and said he would be obliged if Dad would just point the way to the cotton patch.

WWD 2014

Dude Ranching

I TOOK A fall similar to Dad coming off Reece Canyon mesa when I was wrangling horses one summer for a dude ranch in Pennsylvania. I was chasing a horse across an open field and just as I stood up in my stirrups to rope it, my horse stuck a front leg in a groundhog hole and went head over heels in a complete flip. I stayed in the saddle and when it was all over old Jimmy was right side up on his belly and neither of us was hurt but the forks of my saddle were packed full of wet dirt. Evidently, I rolled to one side or the other and had nothing but one leg in the saddle when it buried up in the dirt because I didn't even have a bruise and neither did Jimmy.

That fall was one of the tamer things that happened that summer. Four other Aggies and I signed on when the student aid office at Texas A&M where we were in school advertised for sure enough Texas cowboys to spend the summer wrangling dudes. Red West and I drove up together and got to the place to find about 200 horses that the boss had left word that we were to start riding out to find which ones were kid safe. Between us we got on twenty something horses before we found one that we could un-track without it pitching, throwing some kind of fit or trying to run away. When we got through the string, we had about forty horses that we felt we could put dudes on without getting somebody killed. The other Aggies and the head wrangler, from New Jersey, got there about this time and New Jersey told us to saddle all the horses and to put the boss's saddle – we had yet to meet him – on a big palomino that New Jersey had brought with him. Red and I told him that there wasn't but a handful of horses safe for dudes but he told us "Saddle the horses and don't worry about it". We got the horses saddled just as a Cadillac convertible came roaring up leading three big buses. The bus doors flew open and a mob of kids from three feet tall to teenagers came swarming out. The boss, we found out later that he was the boss's son, got out of his Cadillac and gave a little speech about how much fun the summer was going to be and for everybody to get on a horse. Kids went running to the horses screaming like wild Indians, part of the horses broke loose and took off but we managed to get most of the kids mounted before the boss shouted "Lets ride cowboys" and put his horse

THE GYP LEASE TALES AND OTHER LIES

to a dead run across an open field. The next ten minutes were absolute pandemonium; it was raining kids, horses were bucking and running away, kids were screaming and crying and about twenty or so kids were following the boss at a dead run across the field. He made it about a quarter of the way across before he fell off the palomino and his secretary picked him up in the Cadillac and took him to his living quarters; I didn't see him or the secretary again for a couple of weeks. There were six or eight counselors and a doctor on the buses and between all of us we got the kids gathered up and though I expected dozens of broken bones at the least, none of the kids had anything worse than bumps and bruises. We were two days gathering up horses from all over the country.

We found out later that New Jersey bought all the horses at the Rushville Indiana horse auction starting about a couple of months before camp was to start. The criterion was that it had to be walking and sell for less than seventy-five dollars. As far as I know we didn't have a kid hurt badly all summer but all five of us Aggies got banged up pretty good. The camp hired college kids as counselors but the kitchen help, janitors and maintaince people were all winos off the streets of Philadelphia so the food and accommodations were as bad as you would expect except when the winos stole fruit and sugar from the cook shack and cooked up a big batch of chock beer, then things got real bad. To this day I don't know how those people kept from having kids killed by either the horses or the help but supposedly the camp had been running like that for years.

Calf Roping

LIKE EVERY RANCH kid, I was fascinated by rodeo and at about sixteen set out to become a calf roper. Several of my buddies had similar ambitions and we begged the use of the arena on Double Heart Ranch where Ollie Cox used to produce his Double Heart Ranch Rodeo. We couldn't afford to buy roping calves but we managed to come up with twelve or fourteen Spanish goats and we gathered up at the arena every chance we got to practice our skills. It turns out that our goats did not exactly duplicate the straight runs to the other end of the arena like the calves do at the RCA events. After being roped a few times, their reactions ranged from lying down in the chute and refusing to run at all to dodging side to side and pulling curves tight enough that no horse could follow. The strongest reaction was from the Billy goat, which nobody wanted to draw because his smell would knock, a buzzard off a gut wagon, he would run until he felt the rope settle around his neck and then come back up the rope with fire in his eye and murder on his mind to meet the roper. Rex Brafford was teasing Billy one day, getting closer and closer until Billy charged him and then jumping up on the fence. The fence was heavy bull wire with a thick cable running along the top – Rex would grab that cable and pull up pivoting his middle on the cable to get away. This worked fine until he gripped the cable too hard with one hand and the strands separated to close back up on the skin of his belly when he relaxed his grip. He hung there squalling for a minute until he lost his grip and fell; the cable then pinched four or five chunks of hide out of his belly where the strands closed up. Rex left Billy alone after that.

We scavenged enough material to build a roping arena on Wendell Kent's Dads' place, gathered up enough money and credit to buy some roping calves and four or five of us set out to become calf ropers. It was seven miles from the lot in Sweetwater where I kept Monkey to the roping arena and on roping day I would saddle Monkey, lope a mile and trot a mile out to the arena, rope all afternoon and then ride home the same way. Monkey or I neither one had much fat on us. At this time, calf roping was almost a religion in west Texas; right behind high school football. You could go to one of the little

amateur rodeos that were held somewhere every weekend and there would be 20 or so bareback bronc riders,
10 or 15 saddle bronc riders, 15 or 20 bull riders, 10 or
15 bull doggers and 200 calf ropers. You got two calves
at most shows so only 15 or so people would rope during
the show and everybody else would rope after the show
in what they called "running the slack" and this could go
on until 3:00 in the morning. It's funny but when I got
in college down in southeast Texas, there would be 20
or so calf ropers and 200 or more bull riders at the local
shows. Anyway Monkey and I went through some rough
times, I nearly ruined him by crowding to hard, before
he and I both learned a little bit and we began to make a
fair team. I wasn't winning any money but I usually didn't
embarrass myself and might have made a roper if I had
stayed with it. That's why it smarted when I missed my
first loop roping slack at some little show, caught and tied
with my second loop and the smart mouth announcer
boomed out "Not bad for that kind of roping, a week and
three days."

Trust Your Horse

ONE THING THAT a cowboy soon learns is that many times his horse knows as much or more than he does. Working in the brush – assuming you are riding an experienced brush horse – you have to let the horse pick his own path and do your best not to interfere with his decisions. He is not about to run over that big mesquite tree – that would hurt – so sit easy in the saddle and let him work. The same holds true on trusting the horses' sense of direction. One time we were elk hunting in some rough country way back on the middle fork of the Salmon River. I had tied my horse and gone down on foot into Furnace Creek Canyon. The outfitter and wrangler were going to move camp while we hunted and the wrangler was to meet me at my horse about sundown to take me to the new camp. I misjudged how long it would take me to climb back out of that hole and it was getting dark when I got back to my horse. The wrangler was waiting on me but he was not happy; as soon as I got mounted, he took off like a scalded cat. I didn't know exactly where the new camp was but I knew the general location of where it was supposed to be. When we reached a long ridge near the head of Furnace Creek, both my horse and I thought that we should follow the ridge to find camp. The kid wrangler, however, said that we should go further east and to hurry up because it was getting too dark to see. We went several miles further before he stopped and then took off in a different direction; it was obvious that he was lost as a baby goose. I told him to follow me that my horse would go to camp but by this time, the kid was so spooked that I had to grab his reins and lead him back the way we needed to go. Just as we got back to the long ridge that my horse had wanted to follow the first time we passed it, someone fired a rifle shot just down the ridge and I knew we had found camp. No real damage done but it would be the last time I took directions from the wrangler.

Something that could have been more serious happened when Jack Byrd and I followed some roping calves that got out into a neighbors' pasture that neither of us knew much about. It was late when we went into the pasture and it got dark before we found the calves; we had ridden in half circle looking and I decided to cut across rather than back track the way we had come. It was cloudy and dark as the inside of a barrel but we could keep our directions because we could see the glow of the town lights off to the south. I was going in the direction I needed to go to find the gate when my horse suddenly stopped. I was tired and hungry and I goosed him and said, "Let's go." He didn't move and I was about to set the spurs to him when good sense set in and I loosened the reins and gave him his head. Roany backed up a little and then made a ninety degree turn to the right and stepped off; in a little while he turned back to the left and before long he stopped at the gate. Next day we followed our tracks and found that my horse had stopped on the edge of a twenty foot shear drop into a canyon. We went back to looking for our calves and after a while we rode up on a bluff that over looked the home of the people who owned the ranch. The backyard of the ranch house was right below us and stretched out sunning on blankets on the grass were three teen aged girls, all naked as jay birds. I started backing my horse up and hissing for Jack to "Come on" when Jack booms out, "Hi ladies, how are you all doing?" The girls jumped up and broke for the house and Jack made it worse by calling them each by name as they ran. We still hadn't found our cattle and

I spent more time looking over my shoulder for an outraged father than I did looking for calves but we found our stock and got out without getting shot.

Rough Stock

WHEN I WENT off to school at Texas A & M, I was in the Corps of Cadets and couldn't bring Monkey with me so I joined the rodeo club and took up bareback bronc and bull riding. I realized pretty quick that this was not apt to work out too well; you really need enough coordination to walk and chew gum at the same time if you want to ride rough stock. Anyway being in the rodeo club gave me an excuse to be out of the dorm and away from the sophomores whose mission in life was to make us "fish" miserable so I entered every show that I could. I remember the first bull I got down on, I was shaking like a dog passing peach seeds and the old timer, he was probably 30, helping me said, "Son are you scared?" I said, "Yes Sir", when you are a fish in the Corps, if it moves, you Sir it. He slapped me on the shoulder and said "If you ever get over being scared, don't ever get on another one." The bulls and I didn't get along too well, I don't think I ever rode more than 5 or 6 of the 8 seconds required to be a qualified ride but I did a little better on the bare-back broncs, not good but better. The rodeo stock con-tractors working amateur rodeos in the area did not have exactly the same quality horses and bulls that you see in PRCA events on television. Most of the bulls were all right, lots of Brahman type cattle in southeast Texas, but the bareback horses and saddle broncs left quite a bit to be desired. One bareback horse that I have vivid memo-ries of would not buck at all but would break out of the chute and run as hard as he could for the back fence of the arena. Ten feet from the fence and still going full tilt, he would stick both front feet in the ground and I never saw anybody stay on through this little stunt. The cow-boys hated him but they kept him in the string because he pleased the crowd. Most of the crowd doesn't want to see anybody hurt but the wrecks are what sell tickets. I bucked off a bareback horse one night and landed flat of my back under the horse. I looked up and could see that horse coming down for what seemed like a week but I couldn't get out of the way. When he finally came down it was to put a front hoof on each of my shoulders and a rear hoof on each of my legs; as I lay there dying, I heard a lady in the crowd say "They shouldn't let those boys do that" I wanted to agree with her but couldn't find the wind to tell her so. To make it worse, when I finally crippled back to the chute, the stock contractor said "Thank you Son" dumb like I said "what for?" and he allowed that he would have hated to see his horse land that hard on the bare ground.

Froze Down Goats

ANGORA GOATS ARE probably the most delicate of all domestic animals and they are especially vulnerable right after they have been sheared. When six months or more growth of hair is clipped off it is like stripping a person naked that has been wearing two sets of britches, long handles and a heavy coat all winter and kicking him outdoors. We had sheared goats one spring at the Decker ranch and sorted off a bunch of nannies that Dad wanted to sell. The keeper goats we turned out in a rough pasture with good weather protection and kept the sale goats up in the pens waiting for the trucks to come. Prior to the days of cell phones most ranchers would tell you that they have spent more hours waiting on the trucks that, "will damn sure be there by daylight", then they have gathering the stock to put in the trucks. Anyway we waited around for several hours past when the truck was due and finally started to town to see what was wrong. Just before we got to town, we looked back to see a sight that normally would tickle a dry country rancher pink; a tremendous thunder storm was boiling up right over the ranch and the sky was blue-green with hail. Dad stopped at the house to call about the truck and I raided Mothers pantry for five pounds of sugar and then went to the garage for a five gallon bucket and the gallon of moonshine whiskey that one of our neighbors in Oklahoma had given Dad. We set speed records getting back to the ranch and sure enough could hear the pitiful bleats of chilled down goats even before we got to the pens. The rain was over but there was still ice on the ground from the hail and the temperature must have dropped twenty degrees. Every goat that we had left in the pen was down with her head curled back and most were not even struggling. It looked hopeless but we built a fire and started water heating and then added the sugar and moonshine to make a king sized batch of hot toddies. We went around drenching goats with four ounces of this mixture and the dosed goats began to get up. I have never seen a frozen down goat get up before or since this but we got every goat up and didn't lose a one. Maybe a dozen goats took a second drink before getting on their feet but those got up looking for a bobcat to whip.

I don't know what I would do today if I had chilled down goats; I haven't seen moonshine whiskey in twenty years. When we went to southeast Oklahoma in the early fifties, moonshine whiskey was a cottage industry for lots of folks. For some it was a family tradition going back several generations and some of these people produced whiskey as good as any bonded Kentucky bourbon and took real pride in their product. One family thirty miles east of the ranch made, aged and sold 3,6 and 8-year-old bourbon with their name on the label. Most of the whiskey made, however, was of a little lower quality. Dad said that when he was in college, he saw a lot of whiskey tested by pouring a little out on a porcelain tabletop and igniting it. If it burned with a bright blue flame and didn't leave a black residue, it was judged to be good stuff. If it burned with a yellow flame and left a sooty residue, it was not so good. He saw a lot of whiskey tested but never did see any bad enough for a bunch of college boys to pour out.

I was batching on the Oklahoma ranch in a little house on the banks of Red River when my friend and college roommate, Royce Ginn, came to visit. We had shared a rented apartment with "the Brazos Highwayman", sometimes known as Don Ivey when we were in graduate school at Texas A& M. Royce had lived with me before so was used to eating my cooking even if he did bitch that, "Everything you cook tastes like chili." What he couldn't get used to was the well water; he couldn't drink it straight and could barely choke it down in coffee. One evening we sat down after supper in front of a roaring fire in the fireplace and I poured us both a cup of coffee. Royce took a sip and started in again about how bad the water was; I had a flash of brilliance and said, "Yeah and it's too bad because the well driller hit a vein of the best water you ever tasted just before he drilled into this stuff. I saved a jug of it; let me get you a taste." I pulled a gallon jug of "white lighting" someone had given me out of the cabinet and poured him a paper cup full. Royce took a big slug, made a high pitched whistling noise and his face went red as a beet with tears streaming down his cheeks. For a minute, I thought he was having a heart attack but he recovered enough to look down at what was left in the cup and gasp, "What in the hell is that!" I said, "Local whiskey." He said, "Whiskey hell, gasoline tastes better." and threw the cup into the fireplace where it blew up throwing sparks, coals and chunks of burning wood out into the room. By the time we got all the fire back in the fireplace and put out several little fires in the rug, Royce was over his mad, otherwise, I think he would have thumped my head.

The End for Now

THERE ARE MORE tales to be told but they will have to wait until several more people pass on or at least get too feeble to retaliate against the story teller.